Managing a Community Oral History Project

COMMUNITY ORAL HISTORY TOOLKIT

Nancy MacKay • Mary Kay Quinlan • Barbara W. Sommer

This five-volume boxed set is the definitive guide to all aspects of successfully conducting community projects that conform to best practices in the field of oral history. What are the fundamental principles that make one oral history project fly and another falter? The existing oral history methodology literature has traditionally focused on conducting academic research. In contrast, the *Toolkit* is specifically geared toward helping people develop and implement oral history projects in schools, service agencies, historical societies, community centers, churches, and other community settings. The five concise volumes, authored by leaders in the oral history field, offer down-to-earth advice on every step of the project, provide numerous examples of successful projects, and include forms that you can adapt to your specific needs. Together, these volumes are your "consultant in a box," offering the tools you need to successfully launch and complete your community oral history project.

Volume 1: *Introduction to Community Oral History*, by Mary Kay Quinlan with Nancy MacKay and Barbara W. Sommer

Volume 2: *Planning a Community Oral History Project*, by Barbara W. Sommer with Nancy MacKay and Mary Kay Quinlan

Volume 3: *Managing a Community Oral History Project*, by Barbara W. Sommer with Nancy MacKay and Mary Kay Quinlan

Volume 4: *Interviewing in Community Oral History*, by Mary Kay Quinlan with Nancy MacKay and Barbara W. Sommer

Volume 5: *After the Interview in Community Oral History*, by Nancy MacKay with Mary Kay Quinlan and Barbara W. Sommer

Community Oral History Toolkit

NANCY MACKAY • MARY KAY QUINLAN • BARBARA W. SOMMER

VOLUME 3

Managing a Community Oral History Project

Barbara W. Sommer
with **Nancy MacKay**
and **Mary Kay Quinlan**

Routledge
Taylor & Francis Group

LONDON AND NEW YORK

First published 2013 by Left Coast Press, Inc.

Published 2016 by Routledge
2 Park Square, Milton Park, Abingdon, Oxon OX14 4RN
711 Third Avenue, New York, NY 10017, USA

Routledge is an imprint of the Taylor & Francis Group, an informa business

Copyright © 2013 Taylor & Francis

All rights reserved. No part of this book may be reprinted or reproducedor utilised in any form or by any electronic, mechanical, or other means, now known or hereafter invented, including photocopying and recording, or in any information storage or retrieval system, without permission in writing from the publishers.

Notice:
Product or corporate names may be trademarks or registered trademarks, and are used only for identification and explanation without intent to infringe.

Library of Congress Cataloging-in-Publication Data
MacKay, Nancy, 1945-
  Community oral history toolkit / Nancy MacKay, Mary Kay Quinlan, and Barbara W. Sommer
    5 v. ; cm.
  Includes bibliographical references and index.
  Contents: v. 1. Introduction to community oral history / by Mary Kay Quinlan with Nancy MacKay and Barbara W. Sommer -- v. 2. Planning a community oral history project / by Barbara W. Sommer, with Nancy MacKay and Mary Kay Quinlan -- v. 3. Managing a community oral history project / by Barbara W. Sommer with Nancy MacKay and Mary Kay Quinlan -- v. 4. Interviewing in community oral history / by Mary Kay Quinlan with Nancy MacKay and Barbara W. Sommer -- v. 5. After the interview in community oral history / by Nancy MacKay with Mary Kay Quinlan and Barbara W. Sommer.
  ISBN 978-1-59874-408-8 (complete set - pbk. : alk. paper) -- ISBN 978-1-61132-688-8 (complete set - consumer ebook) -- ISBN 978-1-61132-241-5 (volume 1 - pbk. : alk. paper) -- ISBN 978-1-61132-689-5 (volume 1 - consumer ebook) -- ISBN 978-1-61132-244-6 (volume 2 - pbk. : alk. paper) -- ISBN 978-1-61132-690-1 (volume 2 - consumer ebook) -- ISBN 978-1-61132-247-7 (volume 3 - pbk. : alk. paper) -- ISBN 978-1-61132-691-8 (volume 3 - consumer ebook) -- ISBN 978-1-61132-250-7 (volume 4 - pbk. : alk. paper) -- ISBN 978-1-61132-692-5 (volume 4 - consumer ebook) -- ISBN 978-1-61132-253-8 (volume 5 - pbk. : alk. paper) -- ISBN 978-1-61132-693-2 (volume 5 - consumer ebook)
  1. Oral history--Handbooks, manuals, etc. 2. Oral history--Methodology. 3. Interviewing--Handbooks, manuals, etc. 4. Local history--Methodology. I. Quinlan, Mary Kay. II. Sommer, Barbara W. III. Title.
  D16.14.M22 2012
  907.2--dc23
                    2012026513

ISBN 13: 978-1-61132-247-7 (Paperback)

Contents

Author's Preface | 7

Series Introduction | 9
Defining Oral History | 10
What You'll Find in the *Community Oral History Toolkit* | 11
Best Practices for Community Oral History Projects | 12
Toolkit Contents | 14

1 Introduction | 17
Methodology | 18
Volume Organization | 19
Community Oral History | 19
Sample (Fictitious) Community Oral History Projects | 20
Project Management Process | 22

2 The First Steps | 27
The Basics: Name, Goal, Mission Statement, Focus, and Scope | 28
The Project Design Statement | 29
Ethical Guidelines | 42
Legal Standards | 42

3 People Management | 47
Project Director | 48
Oral History Project Team | 51
Team Recruiting Tips | 55
Team Management Tips | 58
Tips for Working with Volunteers | 63
Project Work Space | 65
Forms and Files | 68

4 Equipment Management | 81
Equipment Options—Overview | 82
Data File Storage and Maintenance | 84
Equipment Kits | 85
Recording Equipment Maintenance Guidelines | 87
Recording Equipment Workshop | 88

5 Money Management | 91
Project Funding and Support Options—Overview | 91
Grants | 94
Donations | 97
Managing a Budget | 99

6 Interview Management | 105
Managing Historical Focus | 106
Ethical Guidelines and Legal Standards | 108
Managing Project Interviews | 110
Interviewer Training Workshop | 117
Repository | 119

7 Winding Up | 123
Immediate Post-Interview Tasks | 124
Managing Preservation | 125
Transcriber Training Workshop | 130
Managing Access | 132
Oral History Management Wrap-Up | 133
Managing Public Relations | 134
Celebration | 136

Appendix Management Survey and Respondents | 139

Notes | 151
Further Reading | 155
Index | 159
About the Authors | 167

Author's Preface

The five volumes of this *Toolkit* take you through the steps involved in designing and carrying out a community oral history project. The information is organized in a sequence that gives you what you need to record interviews with people who are witnesses to or participants in an event or way of life. This volume, Volume 3, lays out the management steps that will help you take a project plan and put it into action to support the interviewing process and complete the project.

Project management is defined as coordinating the activities needed to accomplish a prepared plan. Specifically, oral history project management provides the support structure that surrounds interviews and helps define them as oral histories. It also provides the critical safety net that keeps a project on track and on target.

Throughout this volume, you will see many cross references to our other *Toolkit* volumes. This illustrates the inter-connectedness of all parts of the oral history process and highlights the central role of management in co-ordinating them. Regardless of the size of a project or the number of interviews you may be considering, carefully review this information. It will help you keep your project unified and focused.

I have many people to thank for helping develop this *Toolkit* volume. I have drawn on the expertise of oral history practitioners, whose voices, sent to me in oral history planning and management surveys, are included in this volume. Thank you to Carol Ahlgren, co-director of the Modern Masters Oral History Project, and to Roy Chan, Project Director, Oakland Chinatown Oral History Project, for their review and their comments. Thank you to Mitch Allen, founder of Left Coast Press, Inc. for his support of this project. And thank you to our editor, Stefania Van Dyke, our copyeditor, Louise Bell, and our designer Lisa Devenish. Their editorial and design work is greatly appreciated, both on the individual volumes and on the *Toolkit* as a set of five interrelated volumes. Last, thank you to my co-authors. Work on this volume gave me an opportunity to publish again with Mary Kay and to work with Nancy on a publication for the first time. Our many telephone calls, meetings, and emails strengthened the *Toolkit,* including this volume—*Managing a Community Oral History Project.*

Barbara W. Sommer

Series Introduction

Every community has them. The people who remember

- what happened when the church burned to the ground on Christmas Eve—how the congregation grieved, and then set aside its grief, got to work, and celebrated in a new sanctuary the next year;
- how strangers with pickup trucks took tornado victims to the nearest hospital when a record-breaking storm devastated the community;
- what it was like to bring a neighborhood together to fight the city's plans for a freeway; or
- how children, teachers, and community members felt the first day black and white youngsters shared the same classrooms in the aftermath of all the lawsuits attempting to block school integration.

Old newspaper clippings tell part of the story. So do public records that document the storm, the cost of neighborhood redevelopment, or the text of the court's decision. But what's often missing from the record is the *human* side of the issues, events, and ideas that we call history. And if you're reading the *Community Oral History Toolkit*, there's a good chance you already are thinking like an oral historian. You understand that it's important to add to the historical record first person information that can flesh out or reshape our understanding of past events.

Collectively, we three *Toolkit* authors have spent more than half a century working with community oral history projects, observing along the way how some succeed and others languish. You can readily find an excellent body of literature on oral history methodology, but it is designed for academic research and often does not translate well for unaffiliated community groups. So we've attempted in this five-volume *Toolkit* to identify some fundamental principles that lead to successful community oral history projects and to present practical tools and guidelines that we hope will be useful in a variety of community settings.

Defining Oral History

We define *community* broadly, using the definition found in the Oral History Association's pamphlet *Using Oral History in Community History Projects* (2010). The pamphlet defines community as any group of individuals bound together by a sense of shared identity. For the purposes of this *Toolkit*, we consider community oral history as that being undertaken by any group unaffiliated with an academic institution. Such groups could be neighborhood associations, historical societies, museums, libraries, professional associations, clubs, or any of the myriad ways people organize themselves to accomplish particular ends. Because we consider *community* in its broadest sense, we've included examples of community oral history projects that are diverse in size, topic of study, sponsoring organization, geographic location, and project goals. As you move through your own oral history project, and through the five *Toolkit* volumes, we encourage you to define your own community in the way that works best for you.

Community oral history projects differ in many ways from those originating in an academic setting. They usually

- lack institutional support for planning, managing, or funding;
- are organized around an exhibition, festival, performance, or publication;
- are driven by grant cycles and deadlines, sometimes with a specific goal determined by the funder;
- are carried out by volunteers or by a single paid staff member supervising volunteers;
- barter with local businesses or agencies for office space, technology expertise, and supplies;
- lack infrastructure, such as office space, storage, and computer equipment; and
- almost always have limited funds.

This *Toolkit* recognizes the special challenges community oral historians face and suggests ways to deal with them. It is predicated on the notion that a well-funded institutional setting is not a prerequisite to create solid oral history projects that will endure over time. What is required, however, is a fundamental understanding of oral history as a process that begins long before you ask the first interview question and ends long after you turn off the recorder.

For starters, here's how oral history is defined throughout these five volumes.

> **Oral history** is primary source material collected in an interview setting with a witness to or a participant in an event or a way of life and is grounded in the context of time and place to give it meaning. It is recorded for the purpose of preserving the information and making it available to others. The term refers to both the process and the final product.

What You'll Find in the *Community Oral History Toolkit*

The *Community Oral History Toolkit* consists of five individual volumes. Each volume covers a particular aspect of doing oral history. Although each volume stands alone, the *Toolkit* is best seen as an integrated reference set, in much the same way that any particular aspect of doing oral history is dependent on decisions made at other stages of the process. The *Toolkit* is tightly organized, with subheadings, cross references within the text, and a comprehensive index for ready reference. You'll also find various visual elements, including hot spots (concise tips), definitions, sidebars (case studies and extended discussions), checklists, and figures that illustrate, elaborate, or draw attention to specific points. While all three of us have collaborated throughout the project, we divided the writing duties for the five volumes. Barbara Sommer is the lead author of Volumes 2 and 3; Mary Kay Quinlan is the lead author of Volumes 1 and 4; and Nancy MacKay is the lead author of Volume 5 and overall project coordinator, spearheading the research phase, marshaling the final details and keeping us all on task.

Volume 1. Introduction to Community Oral History. This volume sets the stage for your oral history project. It introduces the field to newcomers, with a discussion of the historical process, the evolution of oral history as an interdisciplinary research methodology, the nature of community and the nature of memory, and the legal and ethical underpinnings of oral history. And as such, Volume 1 importantly lays the theoretical groundwork for the practical application steps spelled out in detail in the subsequent volumes. It also introduces recording technology issues and options for oral history preservation, access, and use. Last, this volume elaborates on our Best Practices for Community Oral History Projects and presents a detailed overview of the remaining *Toolkit* volumes.

> **BEST PRACTICES**
> **for Community Oral History Projects**
>
> 1. **Familiarize yourself with the Oral History Association's guidelines.** First developed in 1968 and revised and updated regularly since then, these guidelines are the benchmark for the practice of ethical oral history and form the foundation on which solid oral history projects are built. Becoming familiar with them will help your project get off to a strong start.
>
> 2. **Focus on oral history as a process.** Keep in mind that, using standard historical research methods, you are setting out to explore a historical question through recorded interviews, giving it context and preserving it in the public record—in addition to whatever short-term goals your project may have such as using interview excerpts to create an exhibit or celebrate an anniversary.
>
> 3. **Cast a wide net to include community.** Make sure all appropriate community members are involved in your project and have an opportunity to make a contribution. Community members know and care the most about the project at hand, and the more closely they are involved in every aspect of it, the more successful it will be.
>
> 4. **Understand the ethical and legal ramifications of oral history.** Oral historians record deeply personal stories that become available in an archive for access both in the present and the future. So oral historians have ethical and legal responsibilities to abide by copyright laws and respect interviewees' wishes while also being true to the purposes of oral history.

Volume 2. Planning a Community Oral History Project. This volume walks you through all the planning steps needed to travel from an idea to a completed collection of oral history interviews. It will help you get started on firm ground, so you don't end up mired in quicksand halfway through your project or trapped in a maze of seemingly unsolvable problems.

Volume 3. Managing a Community Oral History Project. This volume takes the planning steps and puts them into action. It provides the practical details for turning your plans into reality and establishes the basis for guiding your project through the interviews and to a successful conclusion.

Volume 4. Interviewing in Community Oral History. The interview is the anchor of an oral history project. This volume guides the interviewer through all the steps from interview preparation to the follow-up. It includes tips on

5. **Make a plan.** At the outset, define your purpose, set goals, evaluate your progress, and establish record-keeping systems so details don't get out of control.

6. **Choose appropriate technology with an eye toward present and future needs.** Technology is necessary for recording interviews, preserving them in an archive, and providing access and using them for public displays. Make wise decisions about the technology you use.

7. **Train interviewers and other project participants to assure consistent quality.** Oral history interviews differ from some other interview-based research methods in the amount of background research and preparation required. Make sure interviewers and other personnel are thoroughly trained in oral history principles, interviewing techniques, recording technology, and ethics. The *Community Oral History Toolkit* covers all these topics.

8. **Conduct interviews that will stand the test of time.** This is the heart of the oral history process, but its success depends on laying solid groundwork.

9. **Process and archive all interview materials to preserve them for future use.** Oral history interviews and related materials should be preserved, cataloged, and made available for others to use in a suitable repository, such as a library, archive, or historical society.

10. **Take pride in your contribution to the historical record.** Share with the community what you've learned, and celebrate your success.

selecting interviewees, training interviewers, using recording equipment, and assessing ethical issues concerning the interviewer-interviewee relationship.

Volume 5. After the Interview in Community Oral History. Community projects often falter after the interviews are completed. This volume explains the importance of processing and archiving oral histories and takes readers through all the steps required for good archiving and for concluding an oral history project. It finishes with examples of creative ways community projects have used oral histories.

Finally, sample forms, checklists, and examples from the experiences of other community projects are provided that will help guide your project planning and a selected bibliography that will lead you to additional in-depth information on the various topics covered in the *Toolkit*.

We hope you will keep these volumes close at hand as you work step by step through your oral history project. Remember that the effort you put into doing the project right will pay off in unexpected ways far into the future. Many years from now you may well remember the exact words, tone of voice, or facial expression of an interviewee in answering questions only you thought to ask. And you may take satisfaction in knowing that your effort has preserved an important story—a piece of history that gives meaning to all our lives, both now and in the future.

Nancy MacKay, Mary Kay Quinlan, and Barbara W. Sommer

Toolkit Contents

Volume 1 **Introduction to Community Oral History**

Author's Preface
Series Introduction

1. Understanding the Study of History
2. Defining Oral History, Defining Community
3. Special Considerations for Community Oral History
4. Community Oral History Tools and Technology
5. Preserving and Using Oral History Materials
6. Ethical Considerations for Oral Historians
7. Exploring Best Practices for Community Oral History Projects
8. Overview of the *Community Oral History Toolkit*

Appendix: Sample Forms for Managing Oral History Projects

Notes
Glossary
Resources
Toolkit *Index*
About the Authors

Volume 2 **Planning a Community Oral History Project**

Author's Preface
Series Introduction

1. Introduction
2. Getting Started
3. Project Design
4. Planning for People and Infrastructure
5. Equipment Planning
6. All About Money

7. Winding Up

Appendix A: Planning Survey and Respondents

Appendix B: Equipment and Technology Terms

Appendix C: Recording Equipment Standards

Appendix D: Budget and Funding Terms

Notes
Further Reading
Index
About the Authors

Volume 3 **Managing a Community Oral History Project**

Author's Preface
Series Introduction

1. Introduction
2. The First Steps
3. People Management
4. Equipment Management
5. Money Management
6. Interview Management
7. Winding Up

Appendix: Management Survey and Respondents

Notes
Further Reading
Index
About the Authors

Volume 4 **Interviewing in Community Oral History**

Author's Preface
Series Introduction

1. What, Exactly, is an Oral History Interview?
2. Understanding the Ethics of Oral History Interviews
3. Before the Interview: What Project Teams Need to Do
4. Before the Interview: What Interviewers Need to Do
5. During the Interview
6. After the Interview

Notes
Further Reading
Index
About the Authors

Volume 5 **After the Interview in Community Oral History**
Author's Preface
Series Introduction

1. Getting Started
2. Processing
3. Transcribing
4. Cataloging
5. Preservation and Access
6. Winding Up
7. Using Oral Histories

Final Words

Appendix A: Fictitious Project Design Statement, *Project One—Volunteer*

Appendix B: Fictitious Project Design Statement, *Project Two—City*

Appendix C: Fictitious Project Design Statement, *Project Three—Historical Society*

Appendix D: Sample—Legal Release Agreement

Appendix E: Sample—Legal Release Agreement (Restrictions)

Appendix F: Sample Transcript Excerpt

Notes
Further Reading
Index
About the Authors

CHAPTER 1

Introduction

BEST PRACTICE NO. 1

Familiarize yourself with the Oral History Association's guidelines.

BEST PRACTICE NO. 2

Focus on oral history as a process.

BEST PRACTICE NO. 4

Understand the ethical and legal ramifications of oral history.

BEST PRACTICE NO. 5

Make a plan.

You now have followed the advice of Sam Edwards and Lyvonne Chrisman in the nearby sidebar quotation and have developed a plan. The steps covered in this volume take you to the oral history front line for coordinating a project team, creating interview guidelines, training interviewers, learning about recording equipment, and contacting potential interviewees. They underscore our Best Practice No. 5: Make a plan, and serve as a further reminder of our Best Practice No. 3: Focus on oral history as a process. Let's get started.

In some ways managing an oral history project is like managing any other project. It requires a clear mission, a written plan, a realistic budget, a dynamic team, and a strong director. In other ways it is unique because of certain principles embedded in the methodology, such as ethical guidelines, legal standards, interviewing preparation and techniques, and after-

> **A Helpful Reminder**
>
> "The planning processes took place largely in committees and were very critical to the success of the project. Committees identified the goals of the project, formulated methods for getting the work of the project done, carried out the many tasks pertaining to the project.... Far more time was spent in the planning stage than was initially estimated."
>
> *In Our Own Words, The Negro Spirituals Heritage Keepers, Sam Edwards and Lyvonne Chrisman, co-founders, Friends of Negro Spirituals*

the-interview preservation and access steps. Managing an oral history project is a complicated, detail-oriented, and high-energy job. It benefits greatly from consistent leadership—beginning to end—and from committed team members who understand the community, community oral history, and the purposes of the project.

 Managing an oral history project is a complicated, detail-oriented, high energy, and rewarding job.

Methodology

Preparation for writing this volume included a combination of research and hands-on action—literature searches, reading and review of oral history publications and comments on the oral history listserv, attendance at the annual Oral History Association meetings, managing several community oral history projects, and discussions with community oral history workshop participants. All of this helped me think about project management and its importance to oral history in old and new ways.

In addition to research and discussions, I developed a short project management survey as a follow-up to the planning survey of 2009 described in **Volume 2:** *Planning a Community Oral History Project*. In this second survey, I identified oral history management steps and asked for comments about each step. The results of the survey were helpful. Respondents answered questions and gave me tips about what worked and what didn't. I've included their comments in this volume. See Appendix A for a copy of the management survey and a list of participating oral historians.

The *Toolkit* also uses the three fictitious community oral history projects introduced in **Volume 2:** *Planning a Community Oral History Project* to aid the project management discussion. We'll continue to follow them through application of oral history project management steps, analyzing the ways that varying types of community oral history projects can best use these steps.

Volume Organization

This volume is organized around a list of oral history management steps. They are based on the planning steps in **Volume 2:** *Planning a Community Oral History Project* and are designed to translate planning decisions and recommendations into management actions. This list (see pages 22 to 23) is organized in the order project managers are most likely to use the steps, though many, in reality, will be handled simultaneously throughout the duration of a project. Look for in-depth information about oral history interviewing techniques and post-interview archival steps in **Volume 4,** *Interviewing in Community Oral History* and **Volume 5,** *After the Interview in Community Oral History*.[1]

Discussion of the sample forms we developed for use in community oral history projects can be found in Chapter 3. For each form, I follow the same discussion pattern: first I introduce it, then I provide an example filled out with sample information from one of the fictitious oral history projects, and then I use notes to call attention to specific management points that further explain it. Use these samples as guides when developing forms for your project.

This is a hands-on volume. Whether you are running a multiple-interviewer or single-interviewer project, you'll find useful checklists and reminders, examples of completed forms, guidelines on community and interviewee outreach, organizational tips, and comments from oral history project directors about what, in their experience, works for community oral history. And, as with all of the *Toolkit* volumes, at the start of each chapter you'll see several of our Best Practices for Community Oral History Projects. These are reminders of how and where the information in each chapter intersects with and supports the high quality work our Best Practices define.

Community Oral History

Throughout this volume, you will see the terms *oral history, community oral history,* and *community oral history project.* We've included definitions of each in **Volume 1,** *Introduction to Community Oral History* and in our Series introduction. Here's a brief recap for project management purposes.

Oral history is:

- a primary source,
- a recorded interview with people who have first-hand memories of interview topics,
- a copyrightable document, even if copyright is not filed, and
- a document that is preserved and made accessible to future users.

Community, throughout the *Toolkit*, means any group of individuals bound together by a shared identity.

Community oral history is based in the community whose history it documents. Members of the community manage the project and collect its oral histories.

A *community oral history project* is a set of interviews about a defined topic or topics set within the context of a community's history.[2] See Figure 1.1 for an illustration showing community members gathered to learn about oral history.

Sample (Fictitious) Community Oral History Projects

In **Volume 2,** *Planning a Community Oral History Project,* you met three fictitious community oral history projects and learned about how these projects could benefit from project planning. Each project has specific characteristics; together they represent the various types of oral history projects that may be found in communities. Watch for further discussions of these fictitious projects and how they use and benefit from the various management steps in this volume. Here is a brief outline of the three fictitious projects.

Project One—Volunteer: A very small neighborhood oral history project without a budget

Project Two—City: A grant-funded oral history project developed in partnership with a city

Project Three—Historical Society: A pilot project used by an historical society to launch an ongoing oral history program

Project One—Volunteer is relatively informal and probably will take less than a year to complete, including planning time. The project is not affiliated with an institution or organization. Its team will benefit from project management guidance to organize interviews and to contact repositories to finalize preservation and access. Team members will use a Legal Release Agreement developed with help from a law student whose parents are members of the community.

Figure 1.1. Community members gather to learn about oral history. Public Library Genealogy Conference, Oral History Session, Brainerd, MN, 2012. © Barb Sommer

Project Two—City has grant funding, which gives it support and stability. During the planning process, team members discussed how to organize the project scope to meet the grant timeline. The grants organization has specific giving guidelines that dictate some of the interview topics, but the project goals and focus fit well within these guidelines. The project's ties to the city give it a high profile in the community, an asset that can be used when identifying supporters as well as interviewees; however, the project director and team members will need to manage the interviewee choice process carefully to prevent public expectations from dictating who will or will not be interviewed.

Project Three—Historical Society is the first phase of a proposed ongoing program. Its ties to the historical society give it credibility in the community, helping the team members identify supporters and future interviewees. Its ongoing status gives it a sense of stability, and the planners have developed several projects with identified priorities and internal deadlines to further structure this new program. The interviews will be preserved and made accessible through the historical society; a local attorney will help the project director finalize Legal Release Agreement language for this process. The historical society archivist has basic cataloging experience, but will be given specific oral history training and will then be responsible for carrying out the after-interview steps.

> ### Oral History Project or Oral History Program?
>
> An *oral history project* is a series of interviews recorded with a number of interviewees about a specific historical focus; projects have definite end dates.
>
> An *oral history program* is ongoing and often is part of a larger institution such as a library or university; oral history programs include a number of oral history projects within their overall structure.

Project Management Process

Because of the intensity of interviewing and the time commitment needed for interviews, the subject of interviews merit its own discussion. See **Volume 2,** *Planning a Community Oral History Project* for the steps that guide the interview planning process and **Volume 4,** *Interviewing in Community Oral History* for an in-depth discussion of conducting and managing the interviewing process. Revised and refined, these management steps now become our project management guide.

COMMUNITY ORAL HISTORY MANAGEMENT STEPS

- ✓ Choose a project team and director, and define team member roles.
- ✓ Use the Project Design Statement to affirm organization and design.
- ✓ Use the project name, mission statement, focus, and scope as management tools.
- ✓ Be sensitive to oral history ethical guidelines.
- ✓ Apply oral history legal standards.
- ✓ Organize repository/long-term host option arrangements.
- ✓ Finalize and use forms and record-keeping procedures.
- ✓ Finalize and make provision for project space needs.
- ✓ Maintain contact with community supporters and draw on expertise of community resource people.

✓ Decide on recording equipment.
✓ Finalize project budget guidelines and utilize available funding sources.
✓ Finalize orientation and workshop materials and lead training sessions.
✓ Manage interview steps.
✓ Manage after-the-interview steps.

Examining this checklist of management steps in terms of function, you will see that it covers oral history project needs relating to personnel, legal and ethical considerations, project design, infrastructure, equipment, funding, training, interview organization, and post-interview care—the basics of community oral history methodology and of a community oral history project management structure.

 Project management steps define oral history structure.

> ### Excerpt from a Community Oral History Project Interview
>
> "We have faces, we're real people and no two stories are exactly the same. Some of us ended up here [*homeless*] because of misfortune. We're trying to get our lives back together.... I think everybody's story is totally different. There's all sorts of reasons why people are out there doing what they do, their beliefs and things that happen to them."
>
> "Robert," *Your Story and Mine: A Community of Hope Oral History Project.*

Project Management at a Glance

Although each of the steps on the preceding checklist is an important part of a community oral history project, not all of them relate to the interviews in the same way. An understanding of their relationship to one another and to the interviews is critical to project management. Figure 1.2 on the following page illustrates this relationship.

Figure 1.2. Oral History Project Management at a Glance

In this graphic, people—team members, supporters, funders, repository personnel—are represented by the outer structure, while interview-related functions are in the center. This illustrates a basic oral history project management principle or tenet—the work represented by the outer structure supports the interview process.

At the top right of the figure, look for the project planning team. Planning team members were responsible for formulating and developing a project plan including making decisions about name, goal, mission statement, focus, and scope—the basics of oral history interview development. As indicated by the arrows, planning team members could continue to be involved as project team members.

When managing a project, remember that recording oral history interviews is a project end in and of itself.

On the right side, underneath the project planning team, are community advisors and supporters. These are people from the community who can bring specific expertise to a project, raise its profile, and strengthen its ties to the community. Supporters work with the project team but usually do not have direct influence on interview content. They could, however, become project team members and some also might be included as project interviewees.

On the left side of the graphic, starting at the top, are project funders. Funding provides project support but, as indicated by its position on the graphic, does not necessarily have a direct impact on interview content. Underneath funding, with an arrow indicating a direct link to the interviews, are national and state organizations and repository personnel. The organizations provide standards that guide the work of community oral historians; repositories preserve and provide access to oral history interviews.

Looking now at the middle of the graphic and reading from top down, we see first the project team—the people who manage the project and do the interviews. Below the project team, "interview pocess" represents the preparation steps that lead up to doing project interviews. These are the critical steps that manage project focus and define interview content and questions.

The community oral history interviews are in the middle of the graphic. This central position indicates their importance and their relationship to all other components.

Items at the bottom of the figure underneath "community oral histories" are examples of possible project outcomes. Examples include displays and exhibitions, websites, community events, activities, and programs. In many oral history projects, especially community oral history projects, outcomes can be a motivating factor for project organization and may have an impact on interview content. As indicated, they draw on and use information from the oral histories but are not a project necessity.

Remember, as you manage your project, that outcomes are separate from interviews; they come after the oral history process as a distinct set of follow-up activities and events. Recording community oral histories is a project end in itself.

Overall, community oral history project management involves an understanding of oral history and insight into the community. In a survey response, veteran community oral historian Geneva Kebler Wiskemann described it this way: community oral historians should make sure historical focus is clear, a project team has time and energy to do the planned number of interviews, a project has a reasonable and manageable scope, interviewers are trained, team members begin working early with a proposed repository, and the project purpose is clear to the community. These points, reflected in Figure 1.2 and covered in the following chapters, represent the reality of doing community oral history.[3]

CHAPTER 2

The First Steps

BEST PRACTICE NO. 1

Familiarize yourself with the Oral History Association's guidelines.

BEST PRACTICE NO. 2

Focus on oral history as a process.

BEST PRACTICE NO. 4

Understand the ethical and legal ramifications of oral history.

BEST PRACTICE NO. 8

Conduct interviews that stand the test of time.

When the Cushman Motor Works in Lincoln, Nebraska, was approaching its centennial, several long-time employees approached staff members at the Nebraska State Historical Society with an idea. Although the history of the company was well documented, they felt there were few voices in company histories from workers on the production line. As a result, there was little understanding of what working at Cushman meant to people involved with the company. They asked for advice on doing oral history interviews with employees and former employees who assembled the company's classic motors, golf carts, and other products, as a way of celebrating the centennial and including these voices in its history. This idea represented a standard use of oral history—adding previously unrepresented or underrepresented voices to the historical record.

Nebraska State Historical Society staff members helped Cushman employees write a successful grant to the Nebraska Humanities Council for a two-phased oral history project—planning followed by interviewing/management.

The grant allowed project directors to hire two oral history consultants to work with them in planning and managing the project. The consultants led planning sessions, taught interviewer training workshops, helped manage the interviewing process, and oversaw interview transcription. A team of Cushman employees developed the plan, recruited interviewers, identified interviewees, and did the interviews. A second Nebraska Humanities Council grant supported a project outcome—writing a centennial history of the company based on the interview information. The result of project planning, interviewing, and management was a community oral history project encompassing a set of interviews about Cushman Motor Works employee history, now part of the collections of the Nebraska State Historical Society, and a publication, titled *The People Who Made It Work: A Centennial History of Cushman Motor Works*. The project did exactly what the employees asked—it added their voices to the record.

Once the oral history project planners complete a plan and the project moves into the management stage, it is easy to focus on the recordings. After all, interviews are the central purpose for doing oral history. But experienced oral historians understand that overall project management supports doing interviews that, as our Best Practices for Community Oral History Projects state, stand the test of time.

The Basics: Name, Goal, Mission Statement, Focus, and Scope

Volume 2: *Planning an Oral History Project* contains detailed information about planning for the basic community oral history project steps—name, goal, mission statement, focus, and scope. A brief recap follows.

- A project *name*, regardless of the project size, cements its public identity and, in the future, provides a link for access to interview information. The name is used in interviewee correspondence, fundraising, and publicity. The project director and team usually name the project using the name suggested in the project plan.

- A project *goal* is the defined point toward which a project director and team work. As you begin project management, review and, if necessary, refine the goals suggested in the project plan.

- A *mission statement* succinctly defines a project and its purpose. It includes the project name, project focus, and scope, and a statement noting the project is designed and managed according to accepted oral history standards. Creating a mission statement is a planning step; using it to guide development of a project is a management step.

- *Project focus* (historical focus), as explained in **Volume 2,** *Planning a Community Oral History Project,* **Chapter 3,** is the basic interview content statement; it helps guide overall project management.
- *Scope* is a statement about the size and duration of a project.

Taken together, project name, goals, mission statement, focus, and scope form the basic structure that guides oral history project management.[4]

 Creating a mission statement is a planning step; using a mission statement to guide a project is a management step.

The Project Design Statement

The management steps discussed in this volume are common to oral history projects, but the ways communities carry them out are unique to each project. As noted in the Series Introduction for all of the *Toolkit* volumes, community projects differ from projects originating in an academic setting. Within community oral history, management steps also can vary from project to project, depending on size and circumstances. Details about goals, mission statements, numbers of interviews, and types of recording equipment depend on the reality of project needs and resources. This does not imply a change in the standards to which oral historians work; it represents application of the standards to each community oral history project. The care with which this is done depends largely on how a project director and team manage a project.

The Project Design Statement, which was introduced in **Volume 2,** *Planning a Community Oral History Project,* is essentially a project management guide. It lists and defines management steps and summarizes decisions about each. Its use implies acceptance of project design for management purposes. To illustrate how it works, I have filled out three fictitious Project Design Statements, one for each of our fictitious oral history projects. Following each are notes with details about its use for that project.

Project One—Volunteer is a small, short-term project with a goal of collecting oral histories for the community's centennial celebration. It has no source of funding and is run completely by volunteers from within the community. It probably has a team of two or three people and will result in three to five oral history interviews. It does not have ties to a repository, so the project team will have to find a way to preserve the oral histories and make them accessible. It probably will rely on barter and gifts or loans to supply its needs.

Project directors should fill in the Project Design Statement, completing as many items as possible (see Figure 2.1 on the following page). Don't leave lines blank; if something doesn't apply, state this and explain why.

PROJECT ONE MANAGEMENT NOTES

- Always include a mission statement; it is a basic project management guide.
- The administrative requirements section of the form provides a space to include a short description of project team member roles and other information, such as who will develop a Legal Release Agreement for the project.
- The recording plan on this Project Design Statement describes where and how interviews will be recorded, but does not specify the type of video equipment that will be used. When this decision is made, update the form with information about equipment specifications.
- Use the physical space needs section to describe where project materials, including interviews, will be stored until the team turns everything over to a repository.
- Interviewee recruitment information refers to the names of potential interviewees.
- The form has a place to identify repository arrangements. Be as specific as possible with the information included here and revise the form whenever updated information becomes available.

PROJECT DESIGN STATEMENT
GENERAL
PROJECT NAME
Carmel-by-the-Sea (CA) Voices Oral History Project
SPONSORING INSTITUTION
None. This is an all-volunteer project with no institutional affiliation.
PRIMARY GOAL
Team members will conduct 3-5 video interviews with Carmel residents for the city's centennial celebration. Using the interviews, they will produce a centennial celebration DVD.
MISSION STATEMENT
Our community, Carmel-by-the-Sea, California, will celebrate its centennial in three years. This village on the Monterey Bay is known for its old-time charm and for being mostly untouched by the widespread California development of the last half of the 20th century. Through this oral history project, we will explore how and why the city has held out against widespread development. All work will be done to oral history standards.
ADMINISTRATIVE REQUIREMENTS
This is an all-volunteer project run by a team of Carmel residents, one of whom will serve as project director and another as bookkeeper/files manager. Team members are interviewers; each will be paired with a high school student videographer who will be trained on and will use recording equipment from the high school media center. Interviewers will transcribe the interviews. A local attorney will help the team develop a Legal Release Agreement, a local videographer will donate time for a training workshop and for supervision of the students, and an oral history consultant will lead an interviewer/transcriber training workshop for team members and students before they begin recording the interviews.
PROJECT CONTENT
HISTORICAL FOCUS
Urban planning and historic preservation issues in Carmel, CA, during the last decades of the 20th century and the first decade of the 21st century.

(Continued on following page)

Figure 2.1. Fictitious Project Design Statement, *Project One—Volunteer*

Figure 2.1. *Project One—Volunteer (continued)*

SCOPE
Team members will spend 3 months planning the project and then will record and fully process 3-5 interviews with Carmel residents over a 6-month time period. With donated help from a local videographer, they will develop the project DVD after completing the interviews.
TOPICS
Architecture, historic preservation, environment, urban planning, and tourism in the last decades of the 20th century and the first decade of the 21st century.
SOURCES FOR BACKGROUND RESEARCH
Back copies of local newspapers, library files, photographs, city maps, publications about the city, city planning commission and historic preservation board files, California State Preservation Commission files. See the attached project bibliography for detailed information.
PROJECT MANAGEMENT
DURATION
Team members will spend 3 months planning the project and 6 months recording and processing the interviews.
NUMBER OF INTERVIEWEES
3-5 interviewees. The project will result in 3-5 fully processed video interviews, each 60-90 minutes in length.
RECORDING PLAN
All interviews will be video recorded to capture not only the stories but also places in the city's historic district that, as visual elements, contribute to interview context. Audio back-up will be used to facilitate processing. Team members will work with a local videographer and high school student videographers to plan and record each interview, taking care to visually document the relationship between questions/interview content and visual elements.
PHYSICAL SPACE NEEDS
Team members are working with the local library to develop a plan for data file storage. A local videographer will donate a place, equipment, and expertise to help produce the project DVD.

(Continued on following page)

Figure 2.1. *Project One—Volunteer (continued)*

EXPENSES
Team members and local videographer will volunteer their time. Donations from local businesses will be sought to cover out-of-pocket expenses such as recording media, printing and photocopying, and purchase of blank DVDs. See the attached project budget for detailed information.
RESOURCES
Team members will use equipment from the high school media center to record the interviews and production equipment from the local videographer for the project DVD. Local businesses will be contacted to help cover out-of-pocket costs and the local library is a possible project repository.
INTERVIEWEE RECRUITMENT
Project interviewees will be recruited by team members based on background research. Information about potential interviewees will be kept on Interviewee Recommendation Forms for team review and discussion before a final decision is made.
REPOSITORY PLAN
Team members are working with the director of the local library to develop a preservation and access plan for the master recordings. A copy of the recordings also may be deposited with the city and state planning commissions. If, for some reason, the library cannot care for the master recordings on a long-term basis, team members will approach the state preservation commission to discuss other long-term care options.
ONLINE ACCESS FOR INTERVIEWS
Library personnel will catalog the interviews and make information about the project accessible through worldwide cataloging networks.

Submitted by Jean Culligan, Project Director	**Date** *(Insert date)*
Revised by This form will be revised when final equipment and repository arrangements are made.	**Date** *(Insert date)*

Project Two—City consists of a two-year project to document the history of jazz in a city in the southern United States. The project received a $10,000 grant from the city, but needs to match it with additional funding or in-kind services (services in place of funds). Its team is larger than *Project One—Volunteer*, and the grant, depending on how the proposal was written, may support purchase of equipment, hiring a consultant, and other out-of-pocket costs. The city also may provide in-kind support by assigning a part-time administrative position and a small work space to the project which can be used as grant matches. *Project Two—City* is a closed-ended project and will result in eight to ten oral histories, which will be deposited in the city library for ongoing preservation and access (see Figure 2.2).

PROJECT TWO MANAGEMENT NOTES

- The Project Design Statement has a place to identify the name of the sponsoring institution and support institutions or organizations; this is helpful information for project management and for project and interview context purposes.
- The administrative requirement information provides a place to document details about staff and space needs and how they will be met.
- Summarize project organization and management in the project management section of the form.

PROJECT DESIGN STATEMENT
GENERAL
PROJECT NAME
Jazz Atlanta Oral History Project
SPONSORING INSTITUTION
City of Atlanta, Georgia, with support from the Atlanta Public Library.
PRIMARY GOAL
The primary project goal is to document Atlanta's jazz heritage in the context of Southern musical traditions by conducting historically significant oral history interviews and making them accessible. A secondary goal is to use the Jazz Atlanta Oral History Project as a replicable model for future oral history projects focusing on musical heritage in Southern United States.
MISSION STATEMENT
Through this project, information about the generally undocumented history of jazz in Atlanta in the context of Southern U.S. musical traditions between 1975 and 2010 will be recorded. All interviews will be done to oral history standards.
ADMINISTRATIVE REQUIREMENTS
The project will be administered by a .5 FTE (full time equivalent) project director assigned by the city. The project director will hire an oral history consultant to assist with training, Legal Release Agreement development, and cataloging needs. The city will provide work space and access to a telephone, photocopying, and other basic management needs. A project grant will support purchase of recording equipment, a project computer, and the consultant's salary. Volunteers will do the interviews, the transcribing, and basic preliminary cataloging steps. The library will supply a .1 FTE cataloger to the project; the project director may decide to recruit students in a local university library program or music program as interns to help with various project tasks.
PROJECT CONTENT
HISTORICAL FOCUS
Interviews will focus on jazz traditions in Atlanta, Georgia, in the context of southern U.S. musical traditions between 1975 and 2010. Interviewees will represent a broad perspective of backgrounds in terms of age, ethnicity, musical genre, and personal musical styles.

(Continued on following page)

Figure 2.2. Fictitious Project Design Statement, *Project Two—City*

Figure 2.2. *Project Two—City (continued)*

SCOPE
Project planning will take six months; the project will complete 8-10 fully processed interviews over a two-year period.
TOPICS
Southern jazz traditions, instrumentalists and vocalists working in a Southern jazz tradition and setting, roles of jazz club owners with regard to Southern jazz traditions, the Atlanta Jazz Festival.
SOURCES FOR BACKGROUND RESEARCH
Back copies of newspapers, topic-related files at the Atlanta Public Library and the Georgia Historical Society including historical photographs, personal scrapbooks and correspondence, interviewee biographies and websites, and recordings of interviewee performances. See a project bibliography for detailed information.
PROJECT MANAGEMENT
DURATION
2.5 years including 6 months planning time and 2 years recording and processing interviews.
NUMBER OF INTERVIEWEES
8-10 interviewees; 8-10 fully processed audio interviews, each 60-90 minutes in length.
RECORDING PLAN
Project grant funds will be used to purchase high-grade prosumer audio recording equipment and accessories. Interviews will be recorded in .wav uncompressed format using a lavaliere microphone for each interview participant.
PHYSICAL SPACE NEEDS
The Atlanta Jazz Festival has offered a meeting space for use as a recording studio. The interviews will be conducted in this space or in an interviewee's office or studio. The project headquarters will be in an office in a city government building.
EXPENSES
Major project expenses will be covered by the project grant. Additional needs will be supplied by the city and, to a lesser extent, the city library and donations from local businesses. Volunteers will do the interviews, transcribe them, and do basic cataloging; interns may be recruited to help with transcribing and cataloging. See the project budget for full details.

(Continued on following page)

Figure 2.2. *Project Two—City (continued)*

RESOURCES
The project director will call on local jazz leaders to learn about possible project research materials not generally available to the public. Local businesses and jazz clubs will be contacted to ask for contributions or donations to supplement the project grant and in-kind donations from the city and library. Identification of previously unknown records collections may be an outcome of this project.
INTERVIEWEE RECRUITMENT
Names of possible interviewees will be identified through project research. Leaders in the Atlanta jazz community also will be asked to recommend interviewees. Information about potential interviewees will be recorded on Interviewee Recommendation Forms for use in team member discussion and decisions.
REPOSITORY PLAN
All data files of master recordings and transcripts, copies of transcripts printed on acid-free paper, and all project files will go to the Atlanta Public Library to become part of the library's special collections.
ONLINE ACCESS FOR INTERVIEWS
The project director and oral history consultant will work with library personnel to catalog the oral histories and make them available through standard cataloging networks. By arrangement with the Digital Library of Georgia, team members will help make interviews and transcripts accessible through this online public resource.

Submitted by	Date
Andrea Schmidt, Project Director	*(insert date)*
Revised by	**Date**
One of the interviewees unexpectedly accepted a new position out of the country; the project director and team members will decide how to handle this situation and will update the form accordingly.	*(insert date)*

Project Three—Historical Society represents a local historical society starting an oral history program. The program will consist of a series of projects with an overall goal of documenting the community's history. The project director and team will use the first project to develop a template for later projects. The number of interviews and length of this start-up project will depend on historical organization resources; the goal is fifteen fully processed oral history interviews. Completed interviews will be kept in the historical society's archives. Copies of the transcripts and recordings will be available on the historical society's website and will be contributed to the state digital repository. The project probably will have an ongoing in-kind, part-time management position and a place in the historical organization offices to use as a project headquarters. As an ongoing project, it may have some historical organization baseline funding dedicated to it (see Figure 2.3).

PROJECT THREE MANAGEMENT NOTES

- This is Project Design Statement for a more complex community project but it has the same basic oral history management elements as Projects One and Two; these elements are part of an oral history structure supporting the interviews.
- The Project Design Statement identifies the project name and sponsoring institution, which is helpful for management as well as project and interview context purposes.
- The mission statement for this project lays out its purpose and describes how it fits into the historical society oral history program.
- For this project, administrative information includes identifying the project team, supporters, and fundraising goals.
- As with all projects, the Project Design Statement clearly identifies project content; this information defines both the purpose of the project and the basic structure within which interviews will be recorded.

PROJECT DESIGN STATEMENT
GENERAL
PROJECT NAME   It Takes a Village to Make a City: Duluth (MN) Residents Speak Out Oral History Project
SPONSORING INSTITUTION   St. Louis County Historical Society, Duluth, MN
PRIMARY GOAL   This is the first oral history project in the new St. Louis County Historical Society Oral History Program. The goal is to update St. Louis County Historical Society collections with materials that represent a realistic and balanced representation of the county's history.   A secondary goal is to develop a replicable project that can be used as a template for future oral history projects in this program.
MISSION STATEMENT   Through this program, interviewees representing subcultures and constituencies that have been excluded or underrepresented in written accounts of Duluth and St. Louis County history will be identified and interviewed. The first project will focus on the impact of changes on multi-generational family-owned businesses in Duluth. The interviews will be recorded in audio with video selectively complementing the audio. All interviews will be done to oral history standards.
ADMINISTRATIVE REQUIREMENTS   The project will be staffed by volunteers under the direction of a .15 FTE historical society employee assigned to the project. Members of the historical society board of directors will serve as community liaisons and project advisors. The historical society will provide work space and project support including purchasing recording equipment. The society attorney will develop the Legal Release Agreement.
PROJECT CONTENT
HISTORICAL FOCUS   Overall program focus will include American Indians, businesses, artists, and commercial logging and fishing industries for the City of Duluth and St. Louis County. The first project will focus on the impact of changes on multi-generational, family-owned businesses in the City of Duluth.

(*Continued on following page*)

Figure 2.3. Fictitious Project Design Statement, *Project Three—Historical Society*

Figure 2.3. *Project Three—Historical Society (continued)*

SCOPE
6 months planning followed by a 2-2.5 year pilot project.
TOPICS
Duluth business climate, changes in business climate, development of Miller Hill Mall and its impact on multi-generational, family-owned businesses, other factors affecting multi-generational, family-owned businesses in the city, comments on the future of multi-generational, family-owned businesses.
SOURCES FOR BACKGROUND RESEARCH
City library special collections, Northeast Minnesota Historical Center (St. Louis County Historical Society archive) at the University of Minnesota, Duluth, state historical society, back issues of newspapers, historical photographs, maps, and city land use and planning records. See a project bibliography for a full list of sources.
PROJECT MANAGEMENT
DURATION
The project will have a 6-month planning period followed by a 2-2.5 year interviewing period.
NUMBER OF INTERVIEWEES
15 interviewees; 15 fully processed interviews, each 60-90 minutes in length.
RECORDING PLAN
Interviews will be audio-recorded in .wav uncompressed format. Video recordings will be done using an HD recorder to complement audio as needed. Both recorders will be prosumer-quality and will be provided by the historical society oral history program.
PHYSICAL SPACE NEEDS
Work space and interviewing space will be provided by the St. Louis County Historical Society in The Historic Union Depot in Duluth. Some interviews may be done in interviewees' homes or businesses.
EXPENSES
Many expenses including those for work space, office supplies, and project director will be absorbed by the historical society. The historical society board of directors will help raise funds to meet additional costs identified in the project budget, including equipment purchase costs.

(Continued on following page)

Figure 2.3. *Project Three—Historical Society (continued)*

RESOURCES
The historical society board of directors will serve as liaison between the program and the community.
INTERVIEWEE RECRUITMENT
Interviewees will be identified through project research and information from community members including resource advisors at the historical center/county archive and public library special collections librarian. Information about prospective interviewees will be documented on the Interviewee Recommendation Form for team member discussion and decisions.
REPOSITORY PLAN
Data files containing master recordings of interviews and project transcripts will become part of the collections of the St. Louis County Historical Society at the Northeast Minnesota Historical Center, where they will be cataloged and made available to researchers through all major cataloging networks.
ONLINE ACCESS FOR INTERVIEWS
Information about the project and interview transcripts will be posted on the Northeast Minnesota Historical Center website; through an agreement with the Minnesota Digital Library, recordings and transcripts will be posted on its website.

Submitted by	
Thomas Larsen-Johnes, Project Director	Date (insert date)
Revised by	
No revisions at this time.	Date (insert date)

Each of these three projects is a common type of community oral history project. All are designed to contribute new information about a community to the historical record. How they carry this out depends on how the project directors and teams utilize and manage the information on the Project Design Statement.

Ethical Guidelines

Ethical practice in oral history is guided by the set of national standards. Several decades ago, the Oral History Association (OHA), the national association for oral history practitioners, developed a set of oral history *General Principles* and *Best Practices*. Revised several times, most recently in 2009, these principles and guidelines define basic oral history practitioner standards.

Print them out from the OHA website (http://www.oralhistory.org/do-oral-history/principles-and-practices/) and keep them handy. They cover oral history project management steps including interviewing and post-interview care and, as such, reinforce the standards to which oral historians work.[5]

The Best Practices for Community Oral History Projects included in this *Toolkit* describe a standard developed specifically for community oral historians. Print them out too and keep them handy. They not only support the OHA guidelines, but they also reinforce the importance of standards for communities. Use both sets of materials as ethical guides for project management purposes.

 Make copies of the OHA *General Principles* and *Best Practices* and of the *Toolkit*'s Best Practices for Community Oral History Projects available to all members of the project team.

Legal Standards

As explained in detail in **Volume 2, *Planning a Community Oral History Project*,** an oral history interview is a copyrightable document. Although copyright does not need to be filed, oral history practitioners must clarify ownership of interview content as spoken during an interview. This is done through use of a Legal Release Agreement.[6]

Legal Release Agreements do not need to be lengthy or complicated to serve oral history purposes. They must, however, cover basic copyright control over interview contents and they should clearly provide for interview preservation, as these *Tooklit* examples illustrate (see Figures 2.4 and 2.5). The first example is a standard Legal Release Agreement, the second is for the rare times when an interviewee may request some restrictions on use of an interview for a specified period of time.

 Always keep extra copies of the Legal Release Agreement form with you during an interview.

LEGAL RELEASE AGREEMENT MANAGEMENT NOTES

- This form is written as a deed of gift—a voluntary transfer of property (the contents of the interview) given without payment.
- The mission statement is included on the form to provide project context.
- The language "conveying all right, title, and interest in copyright" meets the legal requirement that copyright transfer must be in writing to be valid.
- The agreement defines interviewee and repository rights to the interview.
- The form has a place for interviewee and interviewer signatures; all interview participants must sign a Legal Release Agreement at the end of each interview.

In rare cases, an interviewee may request that access to an interview be restricted for a period of time. The interviewer and interviewee should discuss this request and determine if it is necessary. If there is no other option for handling an interviewee's need for privacy, use a Legal Release Agreement (Restrictions).

> **SAMPLE—LEGAL RELEASE AGREEMENT**
>
> The mission of the _Jazz Atlanta Oral History Project_
> (oral history project) is to document the history of _jazz in Atlanta in the context of Southern U.S. musical traditions between 1975 and 2010._
> The major part of this effort is the collection of oral history interviews with knowledgeable individuals.
>
> Thank you for participating in our project. Please read and sign this gift agreement so your interview will be available for future use. Before doing so, you should read it carefully and ask any questions you may have regarding terms and conditions.
>
> **AGREEMENT**
>
> I, _Joseph A. Browne_, interviewee, donate and convey my oral history interview dated _(insert date)_ to the _Atlanta Public Library_ *(oral history project/repository name)*. In making this gift I understand that I am conveying all right, title, and interest in copyright to the oral history project/repository. I also grant the oral history project/repository the right to use my name and likeness in promotional materials for outreach and educational materials. In return, the oral history project/repository grants me a non-exclusive license to use my interview through my lifetime.
>
> I further understand that I will have the opportunity to review and approve my interview before it is placed in the repository and made available to the public. Once I have approved it, the oral history project/repository will make my interview available for research without restriction. Future uses may include quotation in printed materials or audio/video excerpts in any media, and availability on the Internet.
>
> | INTERVIEWEE | INTERVIEWER |
> |---|---|
> | Name *(print)* _Joseph A. Browne_ | Name *(print)* _Lane Smith_ |
> | Signature _(sign form)_ | Signature _(sign form)_ |
> | Date _(insert date)_ | Date _(insert date)_ |

Figure 2.4. Sample—Legal Release Agreement

> **SAMPLE—LEGAL RELEASE AGREEMENT (RESTRICTIONS)**
>
> The mission of the __Jazz Atlanta Oral History Project__
> *(oral history project)* is to document the history of __jazz in Atlanta in the context of Southern U.S. musical traditions between 1975 and 2010.__
> The major part of this effort is the collection of oral history interviews with knowledgeable individuals.
>
> Thank you for participating in our project. Please read and sign this gift agreement so your interview will be available for future use. Before doing so, you should read it carefully and ask any questions you may have regarding terms and conditions.
>
> **AGREEMENT**
>
> I, __Wesley A. Z. Jones__, interviewee, donate and convey my oral history interview dated __*(insert date)*__ to the __Atlanta Public Library__ _____ *(oral history project/repository name)*. In making this gift I understand that I am conveying all right, title, and interest in copyright to the oral history project/repository. I also grant the oral history project/repository the right to use my name and likeness in promotional materials for outreach and educational materials. In return, the oral history project/repository grants me a non-exclusive license to use my interview through my lifetime.
>
> I understand that I will have the opportunity to review and approve my interview before it is placed in the repository. My gift and the associated rights are subject to the following restrictions:
>
> _____ May not be made available on the Internet
>
> __X__ Public access may not be available until (date):
> *(insert restriction end date)* _____
>
> _____ Other *(specify)* _____
>
> | INTERVIEWEE | INTERVIEWER |
> |---|---|
> | Name (print) __Wesley A. Z. Jones__ | Name (print) __Charles Wilson__ |
> | Signature *(sign form)* | Signature *(sign form)* |
> | Date *(insert date)* | Date *(insert date)* |

Figure 2.5. Sample—Legal Release Agreement (Restrictions)

LEGAL RELEASE AGREEMENT (RESTRICTIONS) MANAGEMENT NOTES

- This form also is a deed of gift.
- It has the same standard copyright language found in the Legal Release Agreement with the addition of a statement defining interviewee restrictions.
- If you use this form, set a specific end date for lifting the restriction and, in interview file notes, document the reasons for using it.
- A Legal Release Agreement (Restrictions) form may not hold up against requests for interview access made through the Freedom of Information Act or by subpoena.

Start oral history project management by working with the basics covered in this chapter. Once you get these steps organized, you will be ready to move on to the next set of oral history project management responsibilities.

CHAPTER 3

People Management

BEST PRACTICE NO. 2
Focus on oral history as a process.

BEST PRACTICE NO. 3
Cast a wide net to include community.

BEST PRACTICE NO. 5
Make a plan.

Oral history focuses on people. Information recorded during interviews comes from the memories of individuals. Practitioners regularly discuss the roles of interviewers and the relationships between interviewees and interviewers. But interviewers and interviewees are not the only people involved in oral history projects. In this chapter, we will cover management of an oral history project's human resources—the team members that make it work. They include project director, interviewers, equipment specialists, processers, bookkeepers, community supporters, and content advisors.

 Appoint one person as project director to manage the project.

Project Director

Let's begin with the pivotal position in a community oral history project—the project director. This person continues many of the responsibilities of the planning director in maintaining ties with the community and keeping the project on track. The project director should be someone who understands the project mission, focus, and scope and who can, if at all possible, make a commitment to see the project through to its end.

The project director has both external and internal responsibilities. This person is the liaison between the project and the community. He or she oversees community outreach and keeps up with project funding, the interviewing schedule, and the many details that maintain stability and keep momentum in place. Review the following discussion of project director responsibilities for further understanding of the importance of this position.

External Responsibilities

Representing the Project to the Community

Oral history projects often take on lives of their own. People are curious about a process that involves hearing first-hand history, especially when it involves members of their own community. Word can travel fast—there's someone going around with a recorder asking questions. A project director who can provide a public face for the project and answer questions about it during the interviewing phase is an asset. This person keeps the community informed, formally and informally, and maintains consistency in the information provided to community members.

Managing Community Supporters

As in our Best Practice No. 3, community oral history projects should cast a wide net when attracting supporters and should then keep them involved. It is the project director's responsibility to oversee maintenance of the files regarding supporters and to acknowledge supporters often.

> "Our project began with two community meetings. Space and snacks were provided by local restaurant, historical museum and a local business."
>
> Mexican Voices, Michigan Lives (Part II), Diana Rivera, Chicano/Ethnic Studies Librarian, Michigan State University

Internal Responsibilities

Supervising the Project Team

Depending on the size and complexity of a project, a number of people probably will be involved in the project. Regardless of how many or few team members there are, they will look to the project director for leadership and guidance.

Maintaining Overall Project Focus

Consistency in direction is important for oral history projects. Sticking to the project mission statement and interview focus keeps a project on track. Project directors should be prepared to make management decisions that maintain the mission and focus, even if they are not easy or popular.

Repository Arrangements

Checking out and recommending preservation and access options is a project planning step. On the other hand, making a final repository or other long-term storage decision, negotiating an arrangement, and maintaining contact with personnel of the repository or other option are management responsibilities, most often responsibilities of the project director. Another project director responsibility is to update everyone regularly on repository discussions and decisions.

Project Forms

Developing project forms is part of project planning, but overseeing their correct and careful use is a project director's responsibility. Reserve time to review and understand the design and purpose of each form and their application by project team members.

Project Budget

Project directors have budget management responsibilities too. They include keeping track of income or support sources, keeping track of grant and gift income and related expenses, and working with a bookkeeper or accountant to maintain project financial records. The amount of time a project director will spend on budget management will depend on the size and complexity of a project. Some projects will need much more financial and budget management than others. But even all-volunteer projects have costs and value, so, regardless of the size of your project, save some time for project financial records management. See Chapter 5 of this volume for in-depth discussion of budget development and fundraising.

Recording Equipment

The project director's responsibilities regarding recording equipment cover overseeing care, maintenance, and scheduling. Specifically this includes making sure project equipment is in good working order and ready for interviews and that a user and maintenance schedule are in place and up-to-date.

Care for recording equipment and media is critical to the success of a project. The time commitment for this management responsibility will vary, but whatever it is, it's a necessity.

Processing and After-the-Interview Care

Managing processing and after-the-interview care is a complicated, multi-step set of responsibilities, as explained in **Volume 5, *After the Interview in Community Oral History*.** Project directors are responsible for determining what a project needs and getting it done.

Interviewer and Transcriber Training

Another project director responsibility is organizing and scheduling a training workshop for interviewers and another one for transcribers, and then overseeing attendance. These workshops teach skills and serve as a reminder of project standards. They are helpful both for the technical knowledge they cover and the project information they present.

Outreach Plan

Another project director responsibility is managing a project outreach plan. This includes developing publicity about the project (mentioning it by name) and planning a celebration for interviewees, interviewers, and other team members.

Project Director Summary

Oral history projects take time. Practitioners estimate that each interview takes about thirty hours to complete, from beginning to end. Project directors often are also interviewers; when they add the director's responsibilities described here, they increase their project time commitment substantially. But directing an oral history project, while exceedingly time intensive, is one of the most rewarding experiences one can have.

A project director is as critical for small projects as for large ones. Even if you are the only person on a project, make time for project management responsibilities right from the start. This will help you maintain stability and focus as you do your interviews.

> "In every way, the project was time intensive, requiring time … and work that had to be done by individuals and subcommittees outside of the regularly scheduled committee meetings."
>
> *In Our Own Words, The Negro Spirituals Heritage Keepers, Sam Edwards and Lyvonne Chrisman, co-founders, Friends of Negro Spirituals.*

Oral History Project Team

The people involved in an oral history project are its most valuable asset. The interviewees are the stars of the show, but it's the full team that makes a project happen. Recruiting a solid team, defining roles and responsibilities, keeping everyone inspired and on track, and rewarding them appropriately can be one of the most challenging parts of project management.

Project team members may be project planning team members who continue with the project, new team members who join the project, or a combination of the two. Throughout this volume, I refer to this group as the project team or the team.

Team Composition

Team members are community members but roles can vary. In some projects, one or two members fill all the project roles; in other projects, each role is filled by one person. Use the following detailed information about skill sets for interviewers and transcribers to help define and fill these positions and to guide the development of skill-set lists for other project team roles, as needed.

OPTIONS FOR ORAL HISTORY PROJECT TEAM MEMBER ROLES

- ✓ interviewer(s)
- ✓ transcriber(s)
- ✓ recording technician(s)
- ✓ recorder maintenance technician
- ✓ office support
- ✓ bookkeeper/accountant
- ✓ processer/cataloger(s)
- ✓ consultant

As you can see, some roles may involve several people, while others such as a bookkeeper or accountant will involve just one person. In addition, resource people (content advisors) and legal advisors may lend their expertise without becoming part of the project team. Keep track of any contracts and related consulting fees in the project files.

 One person may take on several project team roles.

> "While each person working on the project had specific responsibilities, we also worked collaboratively throughout. Because of the nature of the project and the population we were working with, we believed that our diverse skills, expertise and professional and life experiences complemented each other. Therefore, we worked very closely together and often times our input overlapped each other's."
>
> *Your Story and Mine: A Community of Hope, Michigan Historical Museum, Martha Aladjem Bloomfield, Project Director.*

> "[Chippewa Valley Museum] CVM professional staff and trained community volunteers work on our oral history program. We sometimes engage outside consultants to do some of the interviews. We periodically offer training workshops."
>
> *Chippewa Valley Museum (WI), Susan McLeod, Director*

Interviewer

Interviewers are the most visible and well-known members of a community oral history project team. Interviewers' responsibilities include preparing for interviews and conducting and processing interviews. Well-trained interviewers who take the time to prepare for and thoughtfully record each interview are the heart of an oral history project.

The recommended skill set for interviewers includes the following:

- a willingness and ability to do the necessary interview preparation;
- the ability to be a good, attentive listener (this does not mean being a good storyteller);
- the ability to phrase open-ended questions in ways that encourage thoughtful responses;

- a willingness to be inquisitive and analytical, and the ability to think of follow-up questions in an interview;
- the ability to project a non-threatening demeanor, including the understanding that oral history interviews are not places to ambush an interviewee with pointed or critical questions; and
- the ability to develop a trust relationship with an interviewee and to understand the ethical implications of doing so.

For more information, see **Volume 4,** *Interviewing in Community Oral History.*

Transcriber

Transcribers convert or translate spoken words to the printed page. When recruiting and working with transcribers, remember that it can take up to eight hours to transcribe one hour of an interview. Team members who contribute as transcribers can be paid professionals, volunteers, or interviewers who transcribe their own interviews.

The recommended skill set for transcribers includes the following:

- accurate typing and spelling skills;
- the ability to learn to operate the transcribing equipment;
- the ability to clearly hear electronic sound;
- a broad general background to help understand the purpose of the interviews, the voices on the recordings, and the meanings of the spoken words and sentences;
- the ability to translate spoken words to the printed page with accuracy and attention to detail, including determining sentence and paragraph structure and use of punctuation;
- the ability to learn and understand an interviewee's speech patterns;
- the willingness to adhere to project ethical standards including a commitment not to gossip about the contents of interviews; and
- sensitivity to cultural, educational, and social differences that can have an impact on a transcript.[7]

 Project directors should determine if interviewers will be responsible for transcribing their interviews.

Recording Technician

Recording technicians are the people who record project interviews. Project directors sometimes use an interviewer/recording technician team approach when doing video interviews. Recording technicians can be volunteer or paid, and can be specialists on the community resource list or independent contractors. If using this person as a co-interviewer, make sure the person has received project interviewer training and that interviewer roles are clearly defined.

Recorder Maintenance Technician

Recorder maintenance technicians keep recording equipment in running order and troubleshoot any equipment problems. They can be volunteer or paid. Projects with ties to established institutions or organizations, as in two of our sample (fictitious) oral history projects, *Project Two—City* and *Project Three—Historical Society,* may have access to information/technology (IT) personnel to fill this role. Recording technicians also may fill this role.

Office Support

Office support includes helping with interviewee correspondence, maintaining project files, aiding the project director in keeping track of the status of each interview, and taking responsibility for checking recording equipment kits in and out. Projects with ties to institutions or organizations may be able to fill this role with donated services.

Bookkeeper/Accountant

A bookkeeper or accountant, whether volunteer or paid, in-kind or a donated contribution, keeps track of and manages project funding and support. He or she should provide the project director with a monthly budget statement. If a project has one or more grants, as in one of our sample (fictitious) community oral history projects (*Project Two—City*), this team member keeps track of the grant funds and prepares the required reports. A bookkeeper/accountant also prepares a final budget summary or account of project value when a project ends. If a community oral history project is working with a fiscal sponsor, the project director should ask someone from that organization to fill this team member role.

Trained Processor/Cataloger

A trained processor/cataloger can help with project processing and preparing interview materials for ongoing preservation and access. Look to the local library for a community resource advisor who can provide information about cataloging specifications and other preservation and access needs. Also, check with this person about the availability of cataloging software programs for small organizations. **See Volume 5,** *After the Interview in Community Oral History* for detailed information about these post-interview aspects of a project.

Additional team member options can include the following.

- Legal experts may be part of a project team or they may be among the supporters called on for advice as needed. Project directors, for instance, often call on legal experts to draft or review a Legal Release Agreement.
- Consultants may be part of a project team or may be brought in to provide specific expertise. Project teams often use consultants to lead interviewer and transcriber training workshops. If using a consultant, choose a person with oral history expertise and an understanding of the community and its history.
- Interns may be available to a project through connections with a local high school or college/university. If this is the case, identify the intern's needs and areas of expertise and use the person accordingly.

When identifying team members, look for people who can, if at all possible, make a commitment for the duration of the project. Just as finding a project director who can make this commitment is important to keep a project on track, finding team members who can make the commitment is an important way to strengthen a project. People who stay for the duration provide project stability, continuity, and support.

Team Recruiting Tips

As excited as you and your community may be about your project, finding and recruiting team members who understand the project and are able to make the necessary commitment can take time. People interested in becoming involved in the project will be motivated by what you are doing and why you are doing it. They may come with a strong commitment to preserving community history or, perhaps, with identification or a tie to specific topics. This will give them an incentive to be part of the project, but it could have an impact on how they respond to it. When discussing the project with prospective team members, use the mission statement to let each person know what you are doing, how to get involved, and what project expectations are.

> "The OHP [Oral History Project] is a very collegial group. The Chairman [called project director in the *Toolkit*] is considered first among equals, rather than as a 'boss.' There are monthly membership meetings, with reports. There is also an Operating Committee which meets when business decisions need to be made, consisting of: the Chairman, the Office Manager, the Illustrations Editor, the Readers' Advisory Committee Chairman, the Interview Chairman, and the Technical Advisor. The Office Manager, Office Assistant, Interview Chairman, Illustrations Editor; Editor in Chief, Indexing Chairman, Publicity Writer, Graphic Designer, Transcribers (if members of OHP), all report to the Chairman. The Chairman and the Interview Chairman work together to prioritize Interview Requests and to make assignments among the interviewers; the Interview Chairman oversees the processing of interviews after that."
>
> *Greenwich (CT) Library Oral History Project,*
> *Catherine (Cathy) H. Ogden, Chair*

Then, use the following tips to choose project team members.

- Identify the team member positions needed for the project.
- Let community members know what you need. Speak to community groups, put "help wanted" notices in community newsletters, and pass the word whenever you can. (Note: Use this process for team recruiting, not for identifying interviewees.)
- Write a short description of the role of each team member and use this as a guide when discussing team responsibilities and the required commitment. Descriptions for interviewer and transcriber roles will be the most obvious; use them as templates when developing descriptions for other team member roles.

Look for self-starters—people who, once trained, are internally motivated to do what's asked of them. Others, although they initially may express much interest in a project, often lose interest and leave.

Sample: Team Role Description

Interviewer responsibilities

- Conduct background research on project topics.
- Undertake interviewee-specific research.
- Develop questions.
- Schedule interview.
- Record interview (this can include travel to interview location).
- Complete immediate post-interview tasks as assigned by project director.

With practice, interviewers can learn to accomplish these tasks in about thirty hours per interview.

Transcriber duties

- Review and learn project transcript format.
- Listen to and accurately type an interview, word-for-word.
- Understand and use transcribing style guidelines, including rules for punctuation and paragraphing.
- Use correct spelling, including for proper and place names.
- Audit-edit (check transcript, word-for-word).
- Print a copy of the transcript on acid-free paper. Deliver both the printed and the electronic copies to the project director.

Transcribing is intense, dedicated work. Practiced transcribers expect to spend about eight hours on each hour of a recording.

 Interviewer commitment includes interview prep and after-the-interview tasks.

Seek out a variety of skills—not every project team member will be an interviewer. Some people will want the interaction with an interviewee; others may be more interested in transcribing or in helping with project organizational tasks. Ask prospective team members what their interests are and proceed accordingly. The key to building a productive project team is making sure each member fills the role for which he or she is most suited.

Look for people who understand the time commitment involved. Interviewers, for example, should understand that the time commitment is for more than the interview itself and that you also will expect them to attend project orientations/training workshops. Prospective interviewers who only have time for a ninety-minute recording session probably will drift away. The same is true for transcribers. Those who understand the time commitment will be more likely to see the project through.

In community projects, team members often take on more than one role, or switch roles when needed; this is especially true for small projects. Look for people with a variety of skills to promote this flexibility.

Team Management Tips

Team management is as important as team recruiting. Strong project directors understand the importance of the following pointers.

- Interview team members, discuss team roles and responsibilities, and request references. Then, choose team members who can best fill the needs for each area of responsibility.
- Develop and use project time sheets for all members, paid and volunteer.
- Hold a team orientation, and keep it to one/two hours with plenty of time for questions. Offer food—always an incentive to attend a meeting.
- Define and set clear expectations for everyone on the project team. Clearly identify team member expectations. When you have time limits or deadlines, communicate them in writing as well as verbally.
- Don't overload team members. This should go without saying, but the time needed to prepare for and do oral history interviews may come as a surprise. Keep project responsibilities manageable for team members and watch for signs of burnout.
- Take time to get everyone together without overloading anyone. Regularly scheduled meetings build team friendship and strength. At the meetings, talk about the project, share information, discuss and refine interviewing techniques, and bring everyone up-to-date. And, again, offer refreshments.
- Accommodate and be sensitive to people's needs. Consider setting all-team meetings at dates and times that fit into people's schedules as much as possible.

Letters of Agreement

Letters of Agreement are recommended for use with project team members. The examples here are for interviewers and transcribers (see Figures 3.1 and 3.2, respectively). Both identify team member expectations and clearly state project ethical guidelines and standards. Information on the forms represents *Project Two—City,* the second of the *Toolkit's* three fictitious oral history projects.

LETTER OF AGREEMENT MANAGEMENT NOTES

- Ask each team member to read and sign a Letter of Agreement outlining his or her responsibilities. Ask the project director to co-sign the letter.

- Use the Letters of Agreement to provide clarity for team member responsibilities and roles and to maintain this clarity throughout the project. These agreements are especially useful in making smooth transitions if leadership changes occur during a project.

- Letters of Agreement are not contracts, but a signed Letter could be appended to a formal contract as an agreed-upon statement of duties and responsibilities.

- Use these examples as templates when developing Letters of Agreement for other project team members.

LETTER OF AGREEMENT FOR INTERVIEWER

I, _Lane Smith_____, an interviewer for the _Jazz Atlanta_____ Oral History Project, understand and agree to the following.

- I understand the goals and purposes of this project and understand I represent the oral history project when I am conducting an interview.
- I will participate in an oral history interviewer training workshop.
- I understand the legal and ethical considerations regarding the interviews and will communicate them to and carry them out with each person I interview.
- I am willing to do the necessary preparation, including background research, for each interview I conduct.
- I will treat each interviewee with respect, and I understand each interview will be conducted in a spirit of openness that will allow each interviewee to answer all questions as fully and freely as he or she wishes.
- I am aware of the need for confidentiality of interview content until such time as the interviews are released for public use per the repository's guidelines, and I will not exploit the interviewee's story.
- I understand my responsibilities regarding any archival materials or artifacts related to the interview that the interviewee may want to include in the interview process.
- I agree to turn all interview materials over to the repository in a timely manner and to help facilitate all necessary processing and cataloging steps.

INTERVIEWER	ORAL HISTORY PROJECT
Name (print) _Lane Smith_____	Name (print) _Andrea Schmidt, Project Director_
Signature _(sign form)_____	Signature _(sign form)_____
Date _(insert date)_____	Date _(insert date)_____

Figure 3.1. Sample—Letter of Agreement for Interviewer

LETTER OF AGREEMENT FOR TRANSCRIBER

I, _Judi Smith_____(transcriber) agree to the following.
- Create a verbatim transcript according to style guide provided
- Clearly indicate the interviewee, interviewer, and place and date of the interview at the head of the transcript according to the style guide provided
- Deliver electronic copy in Microsoft Word 2010 or later
- Timeframe for delivery _(insert description of timeframe)_

The transcription process will include (check all that apply):

_X_ Audit-checking the transcript

_X_ A reasonable amount of research for correct spelling of proper names

___ Creating chapter headings

___ Creating a Table of Contents

_X_ Creating an index

___ Other (Specify) _____

The oral history project will provide a list of proper and place names wherever possible to facilitate accurate transcribing.

As transcriber, I understand that all information contained in the transcript is confidential. I agree not to disclose any information contained in the transcript, nor will I allow anyone access to the recording or the electronic files while they are in my possession. I agree to delete electronic files and destroy discs at the instruction of the oral history project or at the conclusion of the assignment.

TRANSCRIBER	ORAL HISTORY PROJECT
Name (print) _Judi Smith_____	Name (print) _Andrea Schmidt____
Signature _(sign form)_____	Signature _(sign form)_____
Title _Transcriber_____	Title _Project Director_____
Date _(insert date)_____	Date _(insert date)_____

Figure 3.2. Sample—Letter of Agreement for Transcriber

Time Sheets

A time sheet is a project and people management tool and, as we will discuss in Chapter 5 of this volume, a budget and funding tool. Develop a time sheet suitable for your project and use it for all project team members, volunteer and paid. Include an hourly wage for the value of all team member contributions, volunteer and paid (see Table 3.1). Use a table like this to keep track of the time each team member spends on the project.

Team Member Time Sheet			
Project Name: Jazz Atlanta Oral History Project			
Team Member Name: Lane Smith			
Team Member Responsibility: Interviewer			
Hourly Wage: Volunteer – value at $50/hour			
Date	Hours Worked	Project Tasks	Notes/Comments
(fill in date)	4	Background research, Joseph A. "Joey" Browne interview	Research covered newspaper review, review of Atlanta Jazz Festival file, and local history publication about Atlanta Jazz Festival at Atlanta Public Library

Table 3.1. Sample—Team Member Time Sheet

 Use time sheets for all team members, volunteer and paid.

Project Orientation

When a project team is in place, schedule an orientation. This is not an interviewer or transcriber training workshop; it is a basic project introduction presented to team members by the project director. In this orientation, identify the project by name and give each team member a copy of the mission statement. Discuss the project purpose, goals, mission, focus, scope, as well as project team responsibilities and expectations, ethics, privacy policies, and deadlines. Include free time to give team members an opportunity to get to know the project director and one another. And offer refreshments as part of the encouragement to attend.

> **Suggested Project Orientation Agenda**
> - Introductions
> - Provide basic project description
> - Review project purpose, goals, focus, scope, and mission statement
> - Review ethical guidelines and legal standards
> - Discuss team member roles
> - Provide a brief introduction to the interviewing process
> - Questions

Supporters

Communities are full of talent. As shown in Figure 1.2, supporters may or may not be part of the team, but don't forget that they can provide essential skills and knowledge for the project. In addition to team member management, remember to keep in contact with project supporters. Meet with them, and let them know how things are going. Identify ways in which they can continue to be involved. And thank them—privately and publicly.

Tips for Working with Volunteers

Providing a welcoming atmosphere and rewarding volunteers for their help are essentials in a community oral history project. Catherine H. Ogden, Chair of the Greenwich (CT) Library Oral History Project, a volunteer-based project, provided a succinct description of the volunteer management style of this long-standing community oral history project: "volunteer-led; inclusive and collegial; scholarly discipline; desire to be friendly and community-oriented." All of these points are important, but keeping the project inclusive with a collegial atmosphere and a scholarly discipline are key volunteer management strategies. A collegial atmosphere and emphasis on scholarly discipline set the standard for the project management style, while the inclusive tone motivates volunteers to become involved.[8]

Most community oral history projects are run, entirely or in great part, by volunteers. In fact, many community oral history projects would never get done if it weren't for the dedication, expertise, and long hours logged by volunteers. Here are some tips for optimizing the volunteer experience for both the volunteer and the oral history project.

- Treat the volunteer job as any job. Write a job or responsibility description, interview prospective volunteers, check references, and be very clear about duties and expectations. The volunteer will pick up on the spirit of professionalism and respect the importance of the team role.
- When a volunteer is accepted, use the Letter of Agreement to spell out the duties and expectations for the volunteer's role, and ask the volunteer and Project Director to sign it. Projects that use volunteers often also develop a volunteer manual documenting policies and procedures for everyone's use. Include volunteers in meetings and other project activities to make sure they feel part of the team.
- Respect each volunteer's existing skills and give all volunteers opportunities to learn new skills if they wish. After all, you are getting work done for free.
- Arrange opportunities for honest discussions about each team member's role. These can be monthly conversations with the director or staff meetings. Find ways to give feedback honestly and respectfully.
- Thank the volunteers as often and in as many ways as you can. A party at the end of the season or project, recognition in printed materials, a job recommendation, and a "thank you" every time you see them will go a long way.
- Remember that volunteer rewards include satisfaction in applying expertise, learning new skills, and working in a congenial atmosphere on a worthy oral history project.

> "We have regular membership and committee meetings, a winter holiday party, a spring party jointly with all library volunteers, and a summer [Oral History Project] OHP party to which key library staff are also invited."
>
> Greenwich (CT) Library Oral History Project,
> Catherine (Cathy) H. Ogden, Chair

 Selecting and setting up work space is a management task.

Project Work Space

Volume 2, *Planning a Community Oral History Project,* **Chapter 4** includes a section on identifying project work space needs and making recommendations for basic specifications during the planning stage of a project. Using these recommendations to select and set up a project work area is a management task. This may seem a simple statement, but the importance of having a place to keep project materials in one place, right from the beginning, cannot be overstated.

Project work space does not necessarily mean setting up a project office, though that would be ideal, especially for larger projects. A project work space can be as simple as a desk, computer, and filing cabinet—a place to keep interviews, completed forms, and other materials together, organized, and accessible.

In addition to work space, look also for a place to do project interviews and space to protect and store equipment when not in use. As stated in **Volume 2,** *Planning a Community Oral History Project,* interviewing space should be easily accessible and as free as possible of ambient sound (constant background noise such as running air conditioners or ticking clocks). Storage space for equipment should be secure and accessible to the project team member responsible for scheduling its use.

Once you have a work area, add a few pieces of furniture if you can. Look for a desk or table, a chair or two, filing cabinet, bulletin board or message board, and a bookshelf. Add access to a fax machine and a photocopier, get a project telephone number for a cell phone or land line, and round up some office supplies. Add a computer with dedicated project space, and you are in business. Figure 3.3 illustrates a project work space.

Putting Theory Into Practice

Let's review how the three hypothetical oral history projects could develop a project team and acquire access to work space.

Project One—Volunteer may have one or two core team members, in which case these people will have to cover all of the team responsibilities. Interviews take time; making additional time for project management can overload team members and lead to burnout. Be clear about responsibilities and careful of project team member availability. Consider asking for in-kind support or bartering for personnel needs, such as bookkeeping, transcribing, or cataloging, so the project team doesn't have to do everything. Use time sheets to keep track of volunteer commitment.

Figure 3.3. Listening to and working with community oral history recordings and transcripts in a project meeting room, Liverpool, England, 2008. ©Jennifer Allanson

Team members on this project do not have automatic access to project-designated work space. Consider approaching a local library, local religious institution, historical society, or a local business with a request for a desk and file cabinet. Make sure the space is accessible to team members on a regular basis and that telephone, photocopying privileges, and the like are spelled out. Consider buying donuts or bringing in home-baked goods every once in a while as a thank you.

The reality is that many projects, especially small projects, keep records in someone's home. This often is the most convenient approach during the project, but it can put the interviews at risk after the project ends unless preservation and access plans are clearly spelled out. Don't forget this important commitment.

Project Two—City is a mid-sized, grant-funded project and has more flexibility in providing for project personnel/team needs. Projects like this usually operate with a mix of paid and volunteer staff and team members. A project director can determine which personnel needs the project will hire and pay for and which can be filled by volunteers. In this project, team members probably will be less likely to take on multiple roles.

Additional documentation of project team member responsibilities or job descriptions often is needed at this level, especially if outside funding is involved. And extra paperwork for grant reporting will be needed. The project budget may be more complex, requiring the services of a bookkeeper or accountant to keep track of funding and support, including interim and final grant reports. Depending on the relationship with the city, the project may need a fiscal sponsor to meet grant requirements (see Chapter 5 for details).

This project can benefit not only from grants and gifts of funds, but also from in-kind donations and volunteers. These may, in fact, be necessary: if a local match is needed for a grant award, it often is achieved through the use of in-kind donations and volunteer hours. They add opportunity for additional team member involvement, but expand management responsibilities.

Because of its ties to the city, this project probably will have access to a designated work space that will come with some basic support items: a desk, chair, file cabinet, office supplies, telephone, and photocopying privileges. In a situation like this, ask the project director to clarify the arrangements before beginning the project, and the bookkeeper/auditor to keep track of the value of these contributions.

Project Three—Historical Society is the start of a large, ongoing program affiliated with an institution or organization. Programs like this often have the option to specifically define needs with the understanding the affiliating organization can offer skills or personnel to fill some of them. When developing a program, review team member needs and determine where the affiliating organization can fill in. Then determine which team member roles are ongoing and which may be related to a specific project. Also determine which are volunteer and which are not. For example, the historical society may be able to provide a project director, bookkeeper, and cataloger along with equipment and technical support, while the interviewers could be volunteers assigned to specific projects.

Again, develop responsibility/job descriptions and time sheets for everyone, including affiliated organization personnel. Program volunteers may be listed as the organization's volunteers, but, as mentioned earlier, logging the time they spend on a specific oral history project will allow you to document its value.

As part of an ongoing program, this project probably will have a permanent office space in the historical society with furniture, office supplies, telephone, and photocopying included as part of program support. This is an advantage; it provides program stability at a publicly-recognized headquarters.

Forms and Files

Forms

Project forms are basic management tools for community oral history, and many examples are provided throughout the *Toolkit*. See the full set of sample project forms in the **Appendix of Volume 1,** *Introduction to Community Oral History.* Review the set, choose the forms that work best for your project, and adapt them as needed. The goal is not to inundate anyone with paperwork but to manage the project and the interviews and maintain access to interview information. Ask team members providing office support to keep project forms and files in order.

In addition to the Project Design Statement and the Legal Release Agreement discussed earlier in this volume, the basic project forms described here help maintain management control over a project, including the interviews. Using one of our fictitious oral history projects as an example, let's look at some sample forms and see how they can be used for project management purposes.

The Interviewee Recommendation Form assembles information about potential project interviewees in one place (see Figure 3.4).

INTERVIEWEE RECOMMENDATION FORM MANAGEMENT NOTES

- Use a form like this to help keep track of possible project interviewees.
- Include the full name and any nicknames of the recommended interviewee.
- Clearly state the reasons the person is being considered as an interviewee for the project.
- Use the biographical section to fill in as much detail as possible about the potential interviewee; this information will help you decide whether to interview this person and, if the person is interviewed, it will come in handy in interview preparation.
- Complete the form after a decision about interviewing the person has been made.

 Keep management forms and files up-to-date and accessible.

INTERVIEWEE RECOMMENDATION FORM	
PROJECT NAME Jazz Atlanta Oral History Project	
NAME Joseph A. Browne Also known as Joey Browne	**CONTACT** Director, Atlanta Jazz Festival 246 Peach Street Atlanta, Georgia 30310 404-555-2222 x 1
PLACE OF RESIDENCE 123 Elm Street Atlanta, Georgia 30301 404-555-111 jb@aol.com	**DATE OF BIRTH** April 17, 1955
RELEVANCE TO THE PROJECT (How will this person's life history relate to the goals of the project?) Mr. Browne has been a jazz musician and performer since he was in high school in New York City. He moved to Atlanta to become musical director for the Atlanta Jazz Festival in 1997 and became its executive director in 2006.	
BIOGRAPHICAL SUMMARY (family, education, professional experience, and community activities, as relating to the project) Joseph A. Browne, also known as Joey Browne, was born and grew up in New York City. He graduated from the High School of Performing Arts in 1973 and the Tisch School of the Arts in New York in 1978. He moved to Atlanta to take the musical director position with the Atlanta Jazz Festival in 1997 and was named its executive director in 2006. He agreed to participate in this oral history project because of his background with the festival. He is a trained percussion instrumentalist who studied with Forestorn "Chico" Hamilton and performed regularly with various groups and ensembles at Jazz at Lincoln Center in New York before moving to Atlanta. Since moving to Atlanta, he has performed regularly in Atlanta and in New Orleans. For additional information, see Mr. Browne's resume (attached).	
RECOMMENDED BY Henry D. Petersen, President of the Board Atlanta Jazz Festival	**CONTACT** 404-222-4444, x2 hdp@aol.com
ACTION	
_X_ Approved __Not Approved	**INITIAL MEETING DATE** (insert date)
INTERVIEWER Lane Smith will do this interview.	
INTERVIEW DATE AND LOCATION Atlanta Jazz Festival office (insert interview date)	

Figure 3.4. Sample—Interviewee Recommendation Form

The Interviewee Biographical Profile documents contact information and summarizes interviewee background (see Figure 3.5). It is used for interview preparation and can help establish interview context.

INTERVIEWEE BIOGRAPHICAL PROFILE MANAGEMENT NOTES

- A form like this is useful for interview preparation and for use as interview information; among other things, in the future, it can help provide reliable documentation of the interviewee's background.
- Write in the interviewee's full name, spelled correctly, and common nicknames; use the full name as stated on this form for all other forms for this interviewee.
- Include full contact information; this not only keeps things organized for current project management, it provides identifying information for future reference and research.
- Include biographical information and dates pertaining to interview focus and topics; attach additional information if available and relevant.

INTERVIEWEE BIOGRAPHICAL PROFILE	
PROJECT NAME	
Jazz Atlanta Oral History Project	
NAME	CONTACT
Joseph A. Browne	Atlanta Jazz Festival 246 Peach Street Atlanta, Georgia 30310 404-555-2222, x. 1 jb@aol.com
OTHER NAMES KNOWN BY	DATE/PLACE OF BIRTH
Joey Browne	New York, New York April 17, 1955
PLACE OF RESIDENCE	YEARS IN THE COMMUNITY
123 Elm Street Atlanta, Georgia 30301 404-555-111	Mr. Browne has lived in Atlanta since moving to the city to work for the Atlanta Jazz Festival in 1997.

(Continued on following page)

Figure 3.5. Sample—Interviewee Biographical Profile

Figure 3.5. Sample—Interviewee Biological Profile *(continued)*

OCCUPATION	**EDUCATION**
Jazz musician, arts administrator	Mr. Browne graduated from the New York School of the Performing Arts in 1973 and from the Tisch School of the Arts at New York University (NYU) in 1978. He received his MFA (Master of Fine Arts) from NYU in 1983. He is a jazz percussionist and has studied with Forestorn "Chico" Hamilton.

RELEVANCE TO THE PROJECT
Mr. Browne is a jazz musician and the director of the Atlanta Jazz Festival. In addition to his administrative duties, he regularly performs in Atlanta and New Orleans jazz clubs.
RELEVANT BIOGRAPHICAL INFORMATION (AS IT RELATES TO THE GOALS OF THE PROJECT)
FAMILY (full name, date of birth, relationship to interviewee)
Jane Winter, wife Date of birth: August 10, 1960 Jane Winter met the interviewee at NYU; they married 1983. She originally was from Atlanta, but had lived in New York City while attending the university. Ms. Winter is a professor of history at Georgia State University.
FRIENDS AND ASSOCIATES (full name, date of birth, relationship to interviewee)
Mr. Browne knows most of the jazz musicians in the American South; many serve or have served on the Atlanta Jazz Festival Board of Directors.
PLACES TRAVELED OR LIVED
Mr. Browne regularly travels to New Orleans to perform as well as to New York City several times a year when his schedule allows to perform at Jazz at Lincoln Center.
COMMUNITY ACTIVITIES (Include activity, date, and significance to the project)
Mr. Browne is very involved with the jazz community in Atlanta and in jazz communities throughout the American South. He teaches one class a year at University of Georgia and is in demand as a performer.
INTERESTS
In addition to performing and arts administration, Mr. Browne is interested in the history of jazz in the American South.

(Continued on following page)

Figure 3.5. Sample—Interviewee Biographical Profile *(continued)*

INFLUENCES
Mr. Browne's musical influences are his teachers and mentors, especially Forestorn "Chico" Hamilton. His administrative influences are his Atlanta Jazz Festival Board of Directors.

LIFE MILESTONES
In 2009, Mr. Browne was given a state arts award by the Georgia State Arts Council.

Completed by	Date
Lane Smith, Interviewer	*(insert date)*

The next form shown here, the Interview Summary, is the first interview processing step (see Figure 3.6). It provides immediate control over interview content. Use a form like this to keep track of the following:

- full name, address, and contact information for the interviewee;
- full name, address and contact information for the interviewer;
- date the Legal Release Agreement was signed (it should match the date of the interview);
- information about the interview, including length, format, recording date and place, and any other technical information;
- information about the interviewee and his or her overall response to the interview;
- a list of proper and place names mentioned in the interview, with the notes taken during the interview attached; and
- information about interview content.

INTERVIEW SUMMARY MANAGEMENT NOTES

- Always list the interviewee's name consistently on all forms; add a nickname after the full name if one is commonly used.
- Insert the project name; it will be used as a cataloging identifier for the project from this point forward.
- Include as much detail about the specifics of the interview as possible to provide interview context.

- Use summary statements (bullet points work well) to identify points covered in the interview; catalogers often turn to information like this to help develop access materials.
- This form provides for immediate content control over an interview; the information also is useful for catalogers.

INTERVIEW SUMMARY	
PROJECT NAME Jazz Atlanta Oral History Project	**INTERVIEW ID#** *(insert interview ID number)*
INTERVIEWEE	**INTERVIEWER**
NAME (as it will appear in the public record) Joseph A. Browne 123 Elm Street Atlanta, Georgia 30301	**NAME** Lane Smith 890 Oak Street Atlanta, Georgia 30305
CONTACT 404-555-1111 (home) 404-555-2222 x. 1 (work) jb@aol.com	**CONTACT** 404-666-1111 ls@aol.com
OTHER NAMES KNOWN BY Joey Browne	
INTERVIEW DATE *(insert)*	**INTERVIEW LENGTH** 90 minutes
RECORDING MEDIUM X digital audio __ digital video	
DELIVERY MEDIUM X sound file X sound card __ CD __ DVD	
TECHNICAL NOTES (make/model of recorder, format recorded, microphone notes) The interview was recorded on a Marantz PMD 620 with SD Flash Media using lavaliere microphones.	
INTERVIEW NOTES (physical environment, interviewee's mood, people or animals in the room, interruptions) The interview was recorded in the Atlanta Jazz Festival director's office. Mr. Browne was interested in doing the interview and was prepared for it. He had a number of questions before the interview began and said the topical outline sent to him prior to the interview was very helpful in organizing his thoughts. He was comfortable with the questions asked and added information pertinent to the project at the end of the interview.	

(Continued on following page)

Figure 3.6. Sample—Interview Summary Form

Figure 3.6. Sample—Interviewee Summary Form *(continued)*

DATE LEGAL RELEASE AGREEMENT SIGNED _____   *(date signed/should match the interview date)*
PROPER NAMES AND KEYWORDS   (personal and place names with proper spelling, dates, and keywords)   See the attached list of proper and place names the interviewer jotted down during the interview. Mr. Browne checked the spelling of the names at the end of the interview.
SUMMARY OF INTERVIEW CONTENT   During the interview, Mr. Browne discussed: • His background, education, and early interest in jazz   • His choice of instrument and his musical education   • His description of southern musical traditions   • His musical influences, the roots of some of these influences in musical traditions in the American South, and his thoughts about the influences   • His decision to take a position with the Atlanta Jazz Festival   • The role of the Atlanta Jazz Festival in Atlanta, in Georgia, and in the American South   • Stories of jazz greats who have participated in the festival   • Thoughts about the future of the festival   • Thoughts about the future of jazz traditions in the American South

COMPLETED BY	**DATE**
Lane Smith	*(insert date)*

Project directors also often rely on a form to manage interview processing (see Figure 3.7). The Interview Tracking Form covers the following for each interview:

- names of the interviewer and interviewee;
- date of the interview, date Legal Release Agreement signed (it should be the same date as the interview), and type of Legal Release Agreement signed (general or restricted); and
- project and cataloging information.

Notice that information on the Interview Tracking Form coordinates with Project Design Statement information.

INTERVIEW TRACKING FORM MANAGEMENT NOTES

- The interview identification number at the top of this form is a cataloging step that will be used from this point forward to identify the interview.
- The project name also will be used to identify the project from this point forward.
- When entering the names of interview participants, make sure to spell all names correctly and consistently on all forms.
- Note the option for clarifying permission to release the interview on the Internet.
- Note the specific processing steps and the option to track each one.

INTERVIEW TRACKING FORM		
PROJECT NAME Jazz Atlanta Oral History Project		**INTERVIEW ID#** *(insert interview ID number)*
INTERVIEWEE		**INTERVIEWER**
NAME Joseph A. Browne		**NAME** Lane Smith
CONTACT 404-555-1111 (home) 404-555-2222 x. 1 (work) jb@aol.com		**CONTACT** 404 666 1111 ls@aol.com
INTERVIEW DATE *(insert interview date)*		
DATE COMPLETED	**TASK**	**NOTES**
	Log interview recording and assign an interview ID#	Project volunteer *(name)* working with library cataloger *(name)*; interview is 90 minutes long, data file is saved on sound card, project computer, and external hard drive housed off-site
	Log *Legal Release Agreement*	Project volunteer *(name)* working with library cataloger *(name)*
	Log *Interview Summary*	Project volunteer *(name)* working with library cataloger *(name)*

(Continued on following page)

Figure 3.7. Sample—Interview Tracking Form

Figure 3.7. Sample—Interview Tracking Form *(continued)*

DATE COMPLETED	TASK	NOTES
	Copy recording	City IT personnel *(name)*; follow LOCKSS process
	Label recording media	IT personnel *(name)*
	Transcribe interview	Judi Smith, transcriber
	Audit-check transcript	Judi Smith, transcriber
	Check facts and verify spelling of proper names	Judi Smith, transcriber and Lane Smith, interviewer
	Get interviewee's approval of transcript	Lane Smith, interviewer
	Complete *Cataloging Work Sheet*	Project volunteer *(name)* working with library cataloger *(name)*
	Assemble materials for repository	Andrea Schmidt, project director
	Deliver completed oral history to repository	Andrea Schmidt, project director
	Prepare oral history for website	Library cataloger *(name)*
	Thank interviewee	Andrea Schmidt, project director, and Lane Smith, interviewer
	Archive master files	Library cataloger *(name)*

One of the more interesting things about doing an oral history interview is the additional primary source material that it can bring to light. Interviewees sometimes offer photographs or memorabilia to interviewers. If this happens, the interviewee and interviewer should fill out two copies of the Photograph and Memorabilia Receipt, giving the interviewee one copy (see Figure 3.8). Keep the other copy for the project, and work with the project director and repository to determine the final disposition of the additional materials.

PHOTOGRAPH AND MEMORABILIA RECEIPT MANAGEMENT NOTES
- Use this form as a receipt for items an interviewee may want to loan or donate to the project, with the understanding that further steps are needed to process the materials.

- Use one receipt form for each item or set of items.
- Fill out, sign, and date two copies of the form; leave one with the interviewee and bring one back to the project director.
- Personal interviewee materials such as photographs and memorabilia must not be taken from an interview without a completed, signed, and dated receipt.

PHOTOGRAPH AND MEMORABILIA RECEIPT	
PROJECT NAME Jazz Atlanta Oral History Project	
OWNER	
Name Joseph A. Browne	
Address 123 Elm Street Atlanta, Georgia 40401	**Phone/Email** 404-555-1111 (home) 404-555-2222 x. 1 (work) jb@aol.com
ITEM	
Type Complete set of Atlanta Jazz Festival posters dating from the first year of the festival (1959)	**Quantity** 53 posters
Detailed Description (Describe item and circumstances of loan) Each year the Atlanta Jazz Festival commissions a local artist to create a Festival poster. Poster art work is used on festival materials for that year. This is a complete set of posters dating from the beginning of the Festival. The posters may be scanned for the Atlanta Public Library special collections; they must be returned to Joseph A. Browne no later than two months after this form is signed.	
Associated Dates 1959-2012	
Physical Condition The posters are in full color with some fading on the older posters. All are in excellent condition. Years 1961, 1965, and 1978 have slight tears in the corners where tacks were put through them to hang them on an office wall.	

(Continued on following page)

Figure 3.8. Sample—Photograph and Memorabilia Receipt

Figure 3.8. Sample—Photograph and Memorabilia Receipt *(continued)*

Instructions for use
Credit the Atlanta Jazz Festival and the Atlanta Public Library when using the poster collection; high resolution scans are available from the festival office for publications purposes.

RETURNED	
Items returned by *(name)*: Lane Smith	
OWNER	**INTERVIEWER**
Name (print)	Name (print)
Joseph A. Browne	Lane Smith
Signature	Signature
(sign here)	*(sign here)*
Date	Date
(enter date)	*(enter date)*

Files

Information in project and interviewee files not only defines interview content and context but also documents the project for the community. It also can provide a template for future community oral history projects. Be sure to save all documents related to the project, including completed forms. Project files should include a wide variety of materials ranging from research notes to fundraising materials to interviews. Don't throw away any of the files when the interviews are over; keep them and give them to a repository or secure, long-term storage option, along with the interviews and transcripts.

SUGGESTED MATERIALS FOR PROJECT FILES

- ✓ project mission statement
- ✓ a master list of project interviewees with all contact information
- ✓ a master list of project interviewers with all contact information
- ✓ a master list of other project team members with all contact information
- ✓ a master list of project advisors and supporters with all contact information

- ✓ final project budget statement and supporting information
- ✓ grants management files—projects with successful grant requests need to maintain files according to grant criteria and protocols
- ✓ a master copy of all forms including Legal Release Agreements
- ✓ a list of all project funders and providers of in-kind support with all contact information
- ✓ a copy of project-focused research materials, including packets and timelines developed for interviewer use and a project bibliography
- ✓ a detailed statement about the disposition of project interview recordings, interview transcripts, and all project record
- ✓ project transcribing guide
- ✓ final reports or materials developed by the project director
- ✓ a written assessment of the project developed by the project director

As with the project files, interviewee files contain information documenting content, context, and management and therefore also are an important part of the project record. Those files also should go to the repository or secure, long-term storage option; personnel there will make a decision about what file information is circulating (available to researchers) and what is confidential.

SUGGESTED MATERIALS FOR INTERVIEWEE FILES

- ✓ signed and dated Legal Release Agreement
- ✓ interviewee-specific research materials
- ✓ interviewee correspondence and contact materials including letters, emails, and notes about telephone conversations
- ✓ completed Interviewee Biographical Profile and Interview Summary
- ✓ additional completed forms that relate directly to the interview, such as the project copy of the Photograph and Memorabilia Receipt (including notes about final disposition of the items listed on the receipt)
- ✓ notes written by the interviewer about the interview
- ✓ a master copy of the interview transcript printed on acid-free paper
- ✓ interview-related photographs

Set up a filing system to manage the forms and keep track of remaining project paperwork. Make time to keep the project and interviewee forms and files current and organized. Tasks like this can get lost when you start doing interviews. As experienced oral history practitioners know, managing files keeps track of the information needed during the rest of the project.

Begin using the management information in this chapter as soon as you start a project. Filing system specifics depend on project management decisions. Use the checklists in this section as guides and develop a system that meets your project needs. Regardless of project size, responsible management practices are critical to project success.

Personnel and work space needs, while not always on the top of the list for oral history project managers, have a direct impact on project organization. Small or large, projects that have a strong personnel support structure, a designated work space, and an organized filing system provide a stable structure for doing community oral history interviews.

CHAPTER 4

Equipment Management

BEST PRACTICE NO. 2

Focus on oral history as a process.

BEST PRACTICE NO. 6

Choose appropriate technology
with an eye toward present and future needs.

BEST PRACTICE NO. 7

Train interviewers and other project participants
to assure consistent quality.

BEST PRACTICE NO. 9

Process and archive all interview materials
to preserve them for future use.

Oral historians always seem to have equipment stories; forgetting to turn on the recorder during an interview is one of the most common. But what happens when you turn on the recorder and it doesn't work? This happened recently before an interview with a physician whose specialty expanded rapidly during the last half of the twentieth century. The interviewee was elderly and in poor health, but he had a clear mind and a good grasp of the changes he had witnessed and, in many cases, helped bring about. The interviewers had carefully planned the interview, worked with the physician's son to schedule it, and traveled some distance to interview him in his home. The physician was ready, understood the purpose of the interview, and was looking forward to it. The interviewers checked their recording equipment the evening before the interview and it worked well. They did a sound test the next morning before heading off to the interview and discovered problems. They looked everything over carefully, consulted the recording equipment manual they always kept with the equipment kit, realized this was not a normal troubleshooting problem, and, after about forty-five minutes, tracked down the cause and got everything going. They made it to the interview on time and recorded several hours of first-person information about the history of a particular medical specialty in the United States.

This story isn't included to scare you, though it did scare the interviewers when it happened. The points of the story are:

- the interviewers knew their equipment and were able to troubleshoot on the spot;
- they had read the recording equipment manual and knew where to find answers to their questions;
- their equipment was well-maintained and, in spite of that early-morning glitch, in good working order; and
- they headed off a potentially difficult situation by checking their equipment before they showed up for the interview.

All of these are equipment management steps.

Equipment management is another major area of responsibility for a community oral history project director and project team. Access to good equipment in working order, as the story illustrates, is critical to the success of an interview and a project. This chapter covers equipment options, training sessions, equipment maintenance, and other community oral history project equipment needs.

Equipment Options—Overview

The first question usually asked when discussing oral history project equipment is: Audio or video? See **Volume 2,** *Planning a Community Oral History Project,* **Chapter** 5, for a detailed discussion of using audio, video, or both when recording oral history interviews. To briefly recap, use the equipment recommendations in the project plan as a guide when making your final equipment decisions and choose equipment that works best for your project.

BASIC RECORDING EQUIPMENT FEATURES

✓ sturdy and rugged

✓ good recording/playback quality

✓ user friendly

✓ records and allows interviewers to work in formats that meet oral history standards

✓ relatively lightweight and easy to transport

 Record and preserve oral histories in an uncompressed (audio) or least compressed (video) format.

Recording Equipment

When choosing equipment, if you are working in audio, look for equipment that records in open source, cross-platform, uncompressed format. The equipment should generate data files that can be saved and accessed on a computer and external hard drive. If recording audio on a computer, look for the same specifications.

If you are working in video, look for high definition (HD) equipment that records onto either an internal hard drive or a removable, reusable memory card. Use equipment that allows you to record in the least compressed format possible and in files that can be copied, saved as data files, and accessed on an ongoing basis.

As you review the planning project recommendations, check on the quality of the equipment, including its component parts. Equipment may look good and may generate decent sound, but if it is made with poor quality components, the recordings could deteriorate more rapidly than expected over time. For the latest updates, check Oral History in the Digital Age (OHDA), http://ohda.matrix.msu.edu

Recording equipment accessories are also discussed in **Volume 2, *Planning a Community Oral History Project,* Chapter 5.** Review the lists and recommendations in this chapter for an external microphone and for the additional items oral historians use when recording interviews before acquiring the materials your project needs.

Oral historians use an external microphone to maximize sound quality.

Buy or Barter?

The decision on whether to purchase equipment or use equipment on loan usually is made by the project director in consultation with community advisors and equipment specialists. Recording equipment is expensive and technology changes rapidly. If you decide to purchase, look into package deals that include a recorder, an external microphone, cables, headphones, and a carrying case. If you decide to borrow or lease, check the recorder specifications and how well they will work for your project. Talk with personnel from the repository or long-term storage option, and look into what is realistically available. And, again, don't forget to refer to the oral history equipment guidelines spelled out in **Volume 2**, *Planning a Community Oral History Project,* **Chapter 5** and **Appendix C**.

> **Free, Downloadable Computer Programs**
>
> What about using free downloadable computer programs (Audacity, Gizmo, Facetime, and Skype) or using an iPhone to record project interviews? First, remember that all of these technologies were developed for purposes other than high-quality oral history recording. If you decide to use one for long distance interviews, as an example, carefully examine its recording quality and the long-term preservation and access options. For further helping making this decision, ask for advice and recommendations from repository personnel about various options and the long-term viability of recordings made with each. For sound quality control, stay away from anything that is voice-activated.

Data File Storage and Maintenance

Overseeing preservation and access of interview recordings is a community oral history management step. Preservation and access usually occur in an archival setting—a library, historical society archive, or web host (Internet service that provides website accessibility). This management step requires detailed technical knowledge; if you are working with a repository or archives, you most likely will have found a knowledgeable partner. If you are handling data file storage and maintenance on your own, intending to use a web host, seek out as much information as you can find. At a minimum, be sure the setting you choose has secure, long-term storage management and that your information will be accessible on an ongoing basis. Look for an option that has as much disc space and bandwidth as possible. A server environment that provides back-ups and monitoring checks and maintains data file integrity (checks for data file corruption) is the best choice. And remember, a basic high-definition video recording requires at least six times as much storage space as an audio recording for the same amount of recorded time.

Preserving oral history interviews also involves making multiple copies of recordings and storing them in multiple places. If you use an external hard drive as back-up storage, look for a model that makes conversions and migrations as easy as possible. For detailed guidelines and information about data file storage requirements, see **Volume 2,** *Planning a Community Oral History Project,* **Chapter 5** and **Appendix C** and for information about archival settings, see **Volume 5,** *After the Interview in Community Oral History.*

> To keep up with the latest in data file storage and maintenance, check out these sources:
> - Oral History in the Digital Age (OHDA) guidelines. http://ohda.matrix.msu.edu
> - Baylor Institute for Oral History/Digital Oral History Workshop. http://www.baylor.edu/oralhistory/index.php?id=61236

Equipment Kits

The recording kit and the data file preservation kit are staples of a community oral history project. Assembling one or more recording kits provides your project with the equipment your interviewers need to do project interviews; assembling one or more data file preservation kits allows team members to complete the job.

Recording Equipment Kit

Before your project team begins recording interviews, assemble a recording equipment kit.

SUGGESTED CONTENTS FOR A RECORDING EQUIPMENT KIT

- ✓ recorder
- ✓ AC power cord
- ✓ external microphone
- ✓ microphone cable
- ✓ headphones and cable
- ✓ recording media
- ✓ extension cord
- ✓ paper tablet
- ✓ pencil or pen
- ✓ recording equipment manual
- ✓ set of interview forms

Use each of the items in this kit when recording your oral history interviews. In addition to the recorder, use an external microphone to maximize recording sound quality and maintain flexibility in recorder placement. Cords and cables run the equipment. Interviewers use headphones to monitor sound quality. Media are the devices that hold the sound and video recordings on the recorder. Always include media with extra available recording time in the kit—many oral historians double the anticipated amount of time needed. Digital media are fragile, so also include an extra blank memory card or two. In addition, put fresh batteries in the battery compartment holder of the recorder and another set in the kit if back-up power is needed.

Interviewer support items include a tablet and pencil or pen to take notes during the interview and the recording equipment manual, tabbed, if you want, for easy access to basic care guidelines and troubleshooting options. Include extra copies of the Legal Release Agreement, Interviewee Biographical Profile, Interview Summary, and Photograph and Memorabilia Receipt to have them available during an interview.

Maintaining a recording equipment kit is an ongoing task. Responsibilities include checking the kit before and after each interview, accounting for all items to make sure they are in good working order. Check the media to make sure there is enough recording time for the next interview and that the previous interview has been copied. And do a sound check before putting equipment away and another one before sending it out again. Each of these duties helps keep your kit up-to-date and your equipment in good working order.

Data File Preservation Kit

Douglas Boyd, Director of the Louis B. Nunn Center for Oral History at the University of Kentucky Libraries, recently noted that, with common use of digital recording equipment, oral historians no longer are just collectors of interviews, but have become digital curators the minute they complete each interview. Understanding the basic steps for care of what he described as fragile digital recordings is an increasingly important project management step. As he said, if proper care isn't given the recordings, who knows "if we'll be able to play this stuff in twenty-five years."[9]

To store your recording data files electronically so they will continue to be accessible, use a data file preservation kit.

DATA FILE PRESERVATION KIT

✓ recorder and recording of interview
✓ connector cable (supplied with recorder)
✓ computer and external hard drive

Begin by assembling the recorder, a computer, the connector cable, and an external hard drive. Follow the directions in the recording equipment manual to make the first copy; do this as soon as possible after an interview. Then, using the external hard drive, make several additional copies. Designate one copy as a preservation master (Master Recording) to maintain the interview as recorded with no changes. Once you have completed these tasks, you will have taken the first management step toward becoming the digital curator described by Doug Boyd.

 Your recordings are your project's most valuable products.

Recording Equipment Maintenance Guidelines

Equipment maintenance isn't difficult, but it takes time. A project director or technical advisor usually is responsible for making sure this gets done. Regular maintenance helps assure consistent quality in interview recordings. Keep a checklist and follow it. If you are borrowing or leasing equipment, discuss maintenance and repair responsibilities with the owners, but don't ignore basic equipment care.

MAINTENANCE GUIDELINES

- ✓ Make a list—and a diagram—of recommended recorder settings and keep them with the Recording Equipment Kit; keep copies in the project work space and give them to the technical advisor.
- ✓ Check the recorder after each use; inexperienced interviewers can inadvertently change settings that will affect future interviews.
- ✓ Periodically give the recorder a check-over.
- ✓ Keep a copy of the troubleshooting list from the recording equipment manual in a handy place.
- ✓ Keep careful track of all cords and cables, including the computer connector cable in the data file preservation kit; cables and cords are relatively easy to misplace and are expensive and difficult to replace.
- ✓ Check the microphone periodically to make sure it is working properly.
- ✓ Always keep extra media on hand; digital media are unstable and have been known to fail without warning.
- ✓ Keep an emergency list of contact people with the kit and another copy in the project work place.

Recording Equipment Workshop

Oral history is technology-based. A recording equipment workshop familiarizes team members with the equipment and helps assure consistent interview sound and/or video quality. Project directors sometimes pair a trained equipment operator, especially a videographer, with an interviewer. Workshop attendance by everyone involved with the interviewing process helps all learn information that can have a positive impact on the interview.

Workshops usually are organized by the project director; if you have a technical advisor or experienced videographer available as a community resource person, ask him or her to lead it. Oral historians running small projects may not find it feasible to organize a formal workshop; in this case, seek out technicians or technical advisors and ask for training (see Figure 4.1).

Use the workshop to train team members on how to use the equipment and on the specifics of the interview setting. Review how to set up the equipment, where to place it, and how to monitor it during the interview. If using video, review basic video recording guidelines, including how to set up and frame a shot. Recommend interviewers visit the interview location prior to

Figure 4.1. Equipment training session during The Sound and Story Project Oral History Basics Workshop at the New Rochelle (NY) Public Library, 2011.
©Kristin Charles-Scaringi, Sound and Story Project

the interview to check out sound quality and, if using video, to review the visual setting and check for lighting and sound needs. See **Volume 4,** *Interviewing in Community Oral History*, for more information about an interview setting.[10]

Most recorders and microphones are sturdy and can withstand quite a bit of handling and use. But a basic care and maintenance routine can head off potential problems and keep the equipment running smoothly.

Always remember that equipment is a project tool. Choose items that best meet your needs and are manageable for you and your project team. Anticipate problems and be ready to deal with them, sometimes on short notice. With careful review of the choices and with thoughtful decisions, as well as routine care and management, your project equipment should serve you well.

Suggested Equipment Training Workshop Agenda

- Introduce project director, technical advisor and/or videographer.
- Review project orientation and mission statement.
- Introduce the recording equipment kit—what everything is and what it does.
- Take a close look at recording equipment—how it works.
- Review recording equipment manual.
- Demonstrate how to set up an interview with audio equipment.
- If using video, review video recording guidelines and demonstrate how to set up an interview with video equipment.
- Provide an opportunity for hands-on practice.
- Include the name and contact information of technical advisors.

CHAPTER 5

Money Management

BEST PRACTICE NO. 2

Focus on oral history as a process.

BEST PRACTICE NO. 5

Make a plan.

Let's suppose your community oral history project is entirely made up of volunteers. Is there anything in funding and budget management that can be of help to you? Definitely yes. All projects benefit from analyzing and keeping track of project value, whether it is in the form of grants, gifts, volunteer hours, or in-kind (non-cash) support.

This chapter begins with a short review of oral history project funding and support options. It then turns to general budget management and an overview of grants management. Each of these is as necessary for small projects as it is for large projects. As Elizabeth Haven Hawley, Program Director of the Immigration History Research Center at the University of Minnesota, commented on our management survey, reviewing and maintaining a budget and tracking expenses are important project management responsibilities.[11]

Project Funding and Support Options—Overview

 Funding and support provides stability for oral history interviews.

As used throughout the *Toolkit, funding* refers to monetary sources, whereas *support* encompasses grants but also includes the value of personnel, work space, administrative materials, equipment, file storage, and other oral history project needs. Definitions of various terms relating to funding and support can be found in **Volume 1,** *Introduction to Community Oral History,* **Glossary**. Keep the glossary handy as you read this chapter. See also **Volume 2,** *Planning a Community Oral History Project,* **Chapter 6** for information about budget development and analysis.

> "Time and funding [were important] in the beginning. Time and funding [are important] now. Although we use many volunteers, our staff is responsible for training, supervision, care of the collection and public access to the interviews. This is a research program not a project so we are always considering how to keep going and what to do next."
>
> *Chippewa Valley Museum (WI), Susan McLeod, Director*

Possible sources of funding and support range from local and private sources to national grants. County and state historical societies, local, regional and state libraries, and state humanities councils always are high on the list of funding options for oral history practitioners. Look over the list of sources identified in the project plan and continue to seek out sources that meet your specific project needs.

Funding and Support Tips

Projects can benefit from a variety of types of funding and support. Be creative when thinking about what your project needs are and how you can go about meeting those needs. Beginning with local sources, here are a few ideas.

- Look around the community for places that could help house or provide administrative support for the project.
- Look into community support organizations that offer gifts for community-based projects.
- Check with schools to find out about equipment or services that could be helpful for the project.
- Ask local government officials to write letters of support for the project.

In addition to providing funding or in-kind support, local sources can help in other ways—less tangible but just as important. For example, as these ideas illustrate, they can provide you with valuable community partnerships you otherwise may not know about.

Look also in your state. Get to know the folks at your state historical society and state humanities council and ask for advice.

- State historical societies often have grants programs; check to see if oral history is included as a funding category.
- State humanities councils also have grants programs; check to see if oral history is included as a funding category.
- Ask about other possible oral history funding sources available in your state, such as businesses or foundations that may have an interest in your project focus.

The most common national options for oral history project funding are the National Endowment for the Humanities (NEH), the National Endowment for the Arts (NEA), the National Historical Publications and Records Commission (NHPRC), and the Institute for Library and Museum Services (IMLS). Here are some tips for seeking funding from national sources.

- Check the websites for each to review information that may be applicable to your project.
- National oral history funding is highly-competitive; think carefully about the amount of time it would take to develop a grant proposal, get it funded, and manage it when funded.
- If you have a project that may be competitive at the national level, be sure to explore all your options; ask for advice from the national program on how to proceed and what steps to take next.[12]

> "There was a challenge grant from a local philanthropist for the Bicentennial effort, begun in 1973, and a number of interviews and books were published in that three-year period, in honor of the Bicentennial. According to our interview with our founder, Barbara B. Bloch, when 1977 rolled around, the group decided to continue a good thing, rather than calling it quits. In 1977, the Friends of the Greenwich Library undertook to sponsor and fund the Project."
>
> *Greenwich (CT) Library Oral History Project,*
> *Catherine (Cathy) H. Ogden, Chair*

Grants

Oral history project directors and project teams often seek out various types of support. Even those with an all-volunteer team can benefit from grants, but finding, requesting, and managing them takes time. Grant requests begin with identifying funding guidelines that include oral history and your project focus. Review the materials developed during the planning process and continue the grants work begun with the plan. Grants workshops can be helpful; if you find one in your area, be sure and go. It will help you learn more about grants options and grant writing.

> "The Friends of the Library acted as the project's fiscal agent. The relationships worked well."
>
> *Azusa Heritage Project, Luisa Miranda and Arthur Ramirez, Project Director and Project Videographer/Cameraman*

Projects eligible for grants but lacking a required non-profit status may need to work with a non-profit organization. In cases like this, project directors will want to find and work with a fiscal sponsor, also called a fiscal agent—a non-profit organization that takes responsibility for the finances of an unrelated party. If your project needs a fiscal sponsor, work with your legal advisor to set up and monitor the arrangement.

Figure 5.1, below, is a section from the Minnesota Historical and Cultural Grants Manual. Let's review it as an example of oral history grant writing guidelines and requirements.

MINNESOTA HISTORICAL AND CULTURAL GRANTS MANUAL

Oral History Guidelines

Grants in this category are intended to assist with recording, transcribing, and preserving oral history interviews – focused conversations between a trained interviewer and one or more narrators, capturing information about historical events that can be preserved and made broadly accessible.

Eligible Projects

- Outreach to recent immigrants. Oral history offers the opportunity to include in our public memory the stories of "new settlers" and to welcome them to the broader community.

Figure 5.1. Minnesota Historical and Cultural Grants Manual: Oral History Guidelines *(Continued on following page)*

Figure 5.1. Minnesota Historical and Cultural Grants Manual: Oral History Guidelines *(continued)*

- Military experiences of community members. Sacrifice for country both at home and abroad is a common experience of enduring value.
- Local controversies. Whatever the issue—school consolidation, flood control, town mergers – it is important to capture the perspectives of leaders on all sides of intense public discussions.
- Business developments. A record of economic activity, often underrepresented in reference collections, is critical to understanding any community.
- Natural disasters. In what way do disasters such as floods, lightning strikes or tornadoes shape a community?
- Community life. What are residents' memories of growing up in the community?
- Civic accomplishments. Stories about the significance of place might include demonstrations of local ingenuity or the community pride born of winning a state title in sports.
- Work for the public good. Important contributions to community life are often overlooked in such arenas as public safety (fire, police and other first responders), public service and philanthropy.
- Language preservation. Languages in danger of extinction in Native and immigrant cultures must be captured and nurtured for future use.

What is NOT Funded
- Salvage oral history (interviewing all older people only for their random memories).

Completing the Application
The following advice on how to complete the application will help you shape your project; suggestions are numbered to correspond to sections of the application form and augment guidance provided on the application form.

1. Project Description
- Oral history projects must focus on specific topics, not general experiences. Include a detailed outline of the subject area to be covered in the interviews, including a preliminary draft of the questions to be asked. The result of this project should be transcriptions presenting significant historical information with potential for present and future use.
- Your oral history project must include the use of basic forms such as (1) a donor agreement form that gives you the right to make the transcripts and recordings available for public use at some specified time, and (b) an interview form that provides a record of the vital information of the interview. These forms as well as training in

(Continued on following page)

Figure 5.1. Minnesota Historical and Cultural Grants Manual: Oral History Guidelines *(continued)*

> conducting oral history may be obtained from the Minnesota Historical Society Oral History Office. Include with your grant application copies of the forms you plan to use.
> - Specify what equipment you expect to use to record the interviews, and the source of the equipment.
>
> **2. Need and Rationale**
> - Explain how the project will complement, but not duplicate, existing reference materials on the subject.
> - Why is oral history the proper method for documenting this aspect of history? Will this oral history project allow you to reach out to new audiences?
>
> **3. Work Plan and Timetable**
> - Summarize both the research that has been done and research you plan to do for the project. This section should demonstrate knowledge of the appropriate primary and secondary sources for the project.
> - Explain how your selection of interviewees was made. Keep in mind that a manageable number of interviews is generally less than 20.
> - Transcribe all oral history interviews into typed manuscripts as soon as possible. When developing the work plan, remember that each hour of interview requires approximately eight hours of transcribing time.
>
> **4. Project Personnel**
> - List those who will work on the project, their qualifications and the specific tasks they will carry out. If a transcriptionist or interviewers are to be hired, what qualifications will you require?
> - If possible, state the name of each person to be interviewed, including a brief sentence on why this person is qualified to participate.
>
> **5. Evaluation**
> - Describe your plans for present and future access to the oral histories, including information on any restrictions. Explain how and when the public will access the interviews.
>
> **6. Enduring Value**
> - A duplicate copy of each recording must be made; the copy is to be used for transcribing and for public use. Describe how and where the original recordings are to be stored to ensure their preservation.
>
> **7. Sustainability**
> - Describe the storage areas where the completed oral history tapes, sound files and/or videotapes and the transcripts will be preserved. Include information about security, storage containers and storage climate.

As you can see, the grant guidelines ask for information covered by the oral history project management steps discussed in this volume and summarized in a Project Design Statement. For example, they require that the project topic be defined and explained; this information will be identified in your mission statement and historical focus (see Chapter 2). Note also that projects seeking this community oral history grant must commit to:

- full verbatim transcribing of project interviews,
- use of several basic forms—a donor agreement form (called a Legal Release Agreement in this *Toolkit*) and an interview form (called an Interview Summary in this *Toolkit*), and
- training for the interviewers.

All of these are project management steps. Throughout the guidelines, you will find additional requests for information about project management and project definitions that are covered in this volume. These are common requests: most grant guidelines ask for this type of documentation to assist funders when reviewing grant applications and making funding decisions.

Grants can impose criteria that may or may not fit with your project goals or mission statement, so think carefully about the decision to pursue these funding sources. On the other hand, the money can come in handy and, in some cases, may be necessary to complete a project.

Make sure these funds are spent in a timely fashion, according to the grant guidelines. When a grant is awarded, you probably will be given a management form; use it to keep track of your expenditures along with the amounts and sources of donated funds and in-kind gifts dedicated to the grant. Also, plan on taking time at the end of the project to prepare and submit a final report describing how you used the funds. Grants may be subject to a review, a performance evaluation, and an audit. To meet these demands, you will need the type of information in the sample (fictitious) budget presented later in this chapter, as well as the services of a bookkeeper or accountant and possibly a fiscal sponsor.

Donations

Though grants can be a boon to any oral history project, grant-writing takes time and requires specific skills. Some project directors would rather devote time to conducting interviews, even if it means scaling back. If this is the case, begin planning for meeting needs through partnerships, bartering, and volunteer efforts. Such efforts will contribute to project value and defray costs for some needed items, and they also can help publicize the project and create good will and enthusiasm.

Consider partnerships, bartering, and volunteers as project support options.

Tips for Partnership, Bartering, and Volunteer Support

As in identifying funding sources, be creative when thinking about finding donations for your project. Here are a few ideas.

- Seek a partnership with a local library or business to exchange office space and a phone line for good will and publicity. Consider approaching a local religious institution or community center for office needs; with a mission of community outreach, these organizations may be honored to participate.

- Check high school or community college media centers for a possible loan of recording equipment and/or student technical help. Teachers and outreach coordinators are grateful when real-life projects for students fall into their hands. Not only will you get the technical support, but the students can have a great learning experience.

- Most local businesses welcome an opportunity to be engaged with the community. They are happy to donate goods in exchange for recognition in the project's acknowledgement list. Tap into copy businesses for duplication of transcripts and media, coffee houses and bakeries for refreshments at a project orientation or at workshops, or new photographers who are willing to take pictures of interviewees in exchange for adding the project to their portfolios.

- Skilled expertise can often come for free. Many corporate lawyers enjoy doing pro bono work (work done without compensation for the public good) for projects that interest them; even if a corporate lawyer cannot meet all the project's legal needs, it is an easy way to get started. Law students can provide legal help in exchange for experience. College students can offer expertise, technical skills, and youthful enthusiasm to any project, all for free. Internships, service learning experiences, and independent studies serve the project, the community, and the student.

Community Supporters

Oral history projects, large and small with single or multiple interviewers, also benefit from a network of supporters. These are the volunteers and others who, in addition to the interviewers, meet project needs and are your liaisons to the community. Their gifts of time and talent add to project value.

Community supporters and volunteers are priceless assets.

Always keep an up-to-date list with names and contact information for people who have supported the project. Keep track, with specific dates and times, of the number of hours each has given to the project or the number of times the project director or team members have called on each of them, and include a clear, concise statement about what each supporter has done. Use time sheets to keep track of the time each one gives. All of this is helpful for documenting project support; beyond that, it provides project directors and team members with the information they need to thank project supporters. Let supporters know that, however they are aiding a project, their input adds to overall success. In addition to the budgeted value of their time, they are liaisons between your project and the community.

Managing a Budget

 Monitor funding and support sources regularly.

Now let's look at the specifics of managing an oral history project budget. All projects, even those run solely by volunteers, should have budgets. The numbers will vary, but the categories are essentially the same. Items in each category can represent monetary or in-kind sources, volunteer or paid team members.

In **Volume 2**, *Planning a Community Oral History Project*, **Chapter 6**, We identified and discussed three basic categories for oral history project budget items. These categories provide a structure for analyzing and tracking project funding and support. We'll begin by reviewing each in terms of management responsibilities.

- *One-time or non-recurring expenses.* These are large-ticket items—the recorders, computers, and external hard drives needed to record and preserve interviews. Because they are expensive to purchase, project directors may decide to mix purchase with leasing or borrowing options. Regardless of the choice, document the decision and its value to the project.

- *Overhead costs.* These are day-to-day management items such as paper, pens, photocopying expenses, telephone, and the like. Depending on the resources available to the project, they may be purchased or given

- *Per-interview costs.* These costs will be the most complex to manage and track. Identify all costs related to each interview, including:

  — recording media,

  — travel costs (mileage, meals, and hotels or motels if needed), and

  — time spent on researching and recording an interview.

Sample Budget

The budget discussion in **Volume 2,** *Planning a Community Oral History Project,* **Chapter 6** included a sample oral history project budget. It was developed for a project that had, as an example, a small grant and donations of time and materials. Looking at that same budget, we'll now examine it from a project management perspective (see Table 5.1).

Income

- Cash for this project is less than 10% of total project value. Projects do not need a lot of cash to have a lot of value. The full value of this project is shown as "Total" in the column on the right side of the budget.

- Grant amounts can make a difference. In this budget, a small cash grant is available for one-time expenses such as recorder and accessories, computer, external hard drives, recording media, and transcribing equipment. If a project hires a consultant, cash also could help pay this expense.

- The value of donated contributions and volunteer time add up quickly; these items help defray overhead costs and per-interview costs.

Expenses

- Income should meet or exceed expenses, as it does in this budget.
- The small grant helps this project meet its one-time expenses.
- Large ongoing overhead costs, such as work space, are covered by donations; their value is documented in the project files—the collection of forms, notes and other documents related to the project.
- Interviewers and transcribers are volunteers; the value of their time, per interview, is documented on project time sheets.

(Note: text begins mid-sentence at top: "as donations. Add the purchase price or gift value of each to the budget, taking care to keep notes on the sources of funds and gifts.")

Sample (Fictitious) Oral History Project Budget						
	January	February	March	April	May	Total
Income by Source						
Grants	2,975					2,975
Donations						
Cash	120	85	75	185	50	615
In-Kind	5,280	5,280	5,255	5,255	5,280	25,600
Volunteer	2,000	2,000	2,000	2,000	2,000	10,000
TOTAL	10,225	7,315	7,180	7,290	7,180	39,940
Expenses by Type						
One-Time						
Computer	645					645
Recorder /Accessories		690				690
External Hard Drive, 2@$60				120		120
Overhead						
Office 50sq.ft @$100/sq.ft	5,000	5,000	5,000	5,000	5,000	25,000
Bookkeeping 2hr@$50/hr	100	100	100	100	100	500
Office Help 2hr@$25/hr	50	50	50	50	50	250
Office Supplies	50	50	25	25	50	200
Phtcpy/Pstge	35	35	35	35	35	175
Phone/Fax	45	45	45	45	45	225
Project Packet	45					45
Workshops						
Meeting Costs 2@$75	75		75			150
Manuals $35/mtg	35		35			70
Ldr. Honorarium	100		100		200	
Per-Interview						
Interviewers 40hrs@$50/hr	2,000	2,000	2,000	2,000	2,000	10,000
Transcribing $50/interview hr			400	400	400	1,200
Recording Media 3@$40		80	40			120
Travel @$.55/mile						
Pres/Access Copies	25	25	25	25	25	125
Interviewee Copies	25	25	25	25	25	125
TOTAL	$8,255	$8,125	$7,980	$7,850	$7,730	$39,940

Table 5.1. Sample (Fictitious) Oral History Project Budget

Depending on circumstances, projects with grants or other financial gifts may have to show evidence of in-kind contributions—payments in the form of gifts and services—to balance a cash award. A bookkeeping advisor can help with this task; identifying value on a budget also helps document these gifts.

The budget does not include a figure for a secure, long-term web host for storing interview information. If this option will be used and an annual fee is required, budget a figure for this fee with the understanding that responsibility for the ongoing, open-ended, annual cost will be permanently assigned to someone or someplace before the project ends.

Putting theory into practice

Let's now apply these principles to our three fictitious oral history projects and discuss how they could develop and use various project support sources.

Project One—Volunteer is the small all-volunteer project. It will use a simple budget that includes expenses and covers the value or cost of equipment, of volunteer time for per-interview costs, and of gifts for overhead items such as phone, Internet access, and photocopying.

Project Two—City is the grant-funded project done in partnership with a city. Mid-sized projects like this usually operate with a mix of paid and volunteer team members. The project budget should identify all income and expenses. Expenses for this project include equipment as a one-time expense, team member payments and value of volunteer team member time as overhead and as per-interview costs, value of media and similar items as per-interview costs, and value of donated items that help defray overhead costs. In-kind income given the project in volunteers' time or as overhead items can provide a grants match; a bookkeeper or accountant can provide expertise for this part of grant management, in addition to overseeing general budget management.

Project Three—Historical Society is the pilot project in a historical society oral history program. Large, ongoing programs affiliated with an institution or organization often have the option to work with the organization's accountant or bookkeeper. The project budget may be part of the budget of the larger organization or it may be a separate and distinct budget. The budget for this project will be similar to that for *Project Two—City*. If the project is in a position to receive donated support from the historical society, as well as other grants and gifts, document this donation too.

Supervising the budget and grants, along with documenting gifts of time and materials from supporters, is another project director responsibility. Schedule regular times to work on the budget, keeping track of and analyzing expenses. Identify what you spend, when you spend it, and what you spend it on. Be sure to document gifts of time, talent, and materials; they can offset need for cash.

Keep track of financial, donated, and volunteer contributions and the costs, so you'll know the full value of a project. Track expenses and identify areas where more support may be needed. Document gifts of time, talent, and materials, and assess per-interview costs to determine what it takes in personnel and resources for each interview. Use in-kind and cash donations and volunteer time to match grants as needed; these figures also document the value of links between project and community. All of this information contributes to the bottom line of total project costs and value. At the end of a project, add up all the figures to determine the full cost of your community oral history project. Its value is a gift to the community.

CHAPTER 6

Interview Management

BEST PRACTICE NO. 2

Focus on oral history as a process.

BEST PRACTICE NO. 6

Train interviewers and other project participants
to assure consistent quality.

BEST PRACTICE NO. 8

Conduct interviews that stand the test of time.

BEST PRACTICE NO. 9

Process and archive all interview materials
to preserve them for future use.

One of the five *Toolkit* volumes is dedicated to an in-depth discussion of oral history interviewing: **Volume 4,** *Interviewing in Community Oral History.* In this chapter, I'll review management steps that support community oral history project interviews. As Susan McLeod described in her response to a survey question, oral history interview management takes careful thought as well as sensitivity to community needs.

> "In the first years [of our ongoing oral history program], CVM [the Chippewa Valley Museum] generally interviewed people who were politically, socially or professionally prominent or known to be knowledgeable about a topic of interest. Although we are glad to have these interviews, we rarely find them useful for development of public programming. Now, we generally select a theme and do general background reading and archival research to prepare for interviewing on specific themes or topics. Then we can be sure the interviews will find their way into public programming."
>
> *Chippewa Valley Museum (WI), Susan McLeod, Director*

Managing Historical Focus

Reviewing and finalizing the historical focus in the project plan and then maintaining this focus throughout the interviewing and after-interview process is an important management responsibility. A good beginning for this discussion is the information on defining focus and topics in **Volume 2: *Planning an Oral History Project.***

Reviewing Historical Focus

Look over this information and then review the historical focus proposed in the project plan. Make sure it meets project goals and fulfills project expectations as written in the mission statement. Use the information on the Project Design Statement, especially the Project Content section, to guide the discussion. Discuss the suggested focus with your content advisors—community members knowledgeable about the interviewees and subject matter—and look for research materials that can help you in interview preparation. Although you don't want to start over in your planning process, this is the time to update the plan if needed. Be as clear as you can about the historical focus. It is the basic interview content guideline.

Next, again using your project research, review and define suggested project interview topics. These are the specific subjects or themes within the project focus you will cover with your interviewees during interviews. Think carefully about the topics—they add definition to historical focus and substance to interview content. For example, if a project focus is development of a shopping mall in a community, topics might include information about businesses in the community before the mall was built, memories of the steps that led to building the shopping mall, location of the shopping mall, impact of opening the shopping mall on local businesses, impact of the opening of the shopping mall on the community, and the like. For more information about this process, see **Volume 4,** *Interviewing in Community Oral History.*

After you have reviewed and reached consensus about the project focus and topics, be sure to do the same for the project scope and mission statement. Again, this is not the time to make any major changes in your plan, but a review of these project basics can help you spot any minor revisions that may be needed. Once the goals, historical focus and topics, scope, and mission statement are in place, update the Project Design Statement as needed. Review and discuss this information with the entire project team, covering each item in detail. This is the structure of your project and definition of interview content; it will delineate what interviewers cover in the project interviews.

Maintaining Historical Focus

Managing historical focus doesn't stop with this review, however. It continues as historical focus maintenance throughout the project. Consider what could happen if additional topics come to light during the project. While interesting or potentially substantive, new topics could take your project beyond its defined historical focus. This is a project management situation. Turn to your project basics to help you make decisions that will benefit the project while maintaining historical focus, and document all decisions for your project files.

Interview Context

Oral history interviews do not occur in a vacuum. Context helps define nuance, depth, and meaning of interview information. It provides clues to an interviewee's frame of reference for the interview and may help people using the interview information to understand his or her frame of mind. It also helps define why each interviewee was interviewed by each interviewer at a particular time and place about the historical focus and project topics.

In addition to the Interview Summary, the various project forms and background materials all can contain context information. The project director's management responsibilities include training interviewers to use these forms to document the information. The project director should make sure project and interviewee forms and other file materials are complete and up-to-date and all project files with context information are intact and ready to turn over, in a timely fashion, to a repository or other secure, long-term storage option.

Ethical Guidelines and Legal Standards

Interview management also includes steps relating to ethical guidelines and legal standards that set the tone for the interviews. These steps include making decisions about the interviewer-interviewee relationship, showing respect for the interviewee and the interviewee's memories, and being clear about the purpose and disposition of the interviews.

Managing these steps in a timely and sensitive fashion fosters an open, transparent atmosphere for project team members, interviewees, and community supporters. Some interviewees may need confidentiality; this should not, however, prevent an understanding among team members, interviewees, and supporters about openness in project purpose, goals, interview context and content, and interview disposition.

Legal standards provide the framework that protects interview information and makes it accessible on an ongoing basis. Related management responsibilities begin with an understanding of interview status as a copyrightable document. Project directors are responsible for finalizing the language in a Legal Release Agreement and seeing that project interviewers are trained in its use. For this step, review the information on legal standards in each of the *Toolkit* volumes and in *A Guide to Oral History and the Law*.[13] A repository, if you are using one, is another good source for advice. Project directors also often ask an attorney or law student to help develop the Legal Release Agreement.

LEGAL/ETHICAL CONSIDERATIONS FOR COMMUNITY ORAL HISTORY PROJECTS

✓ Share the information with the community.

✓ Protect against slander and libel.

✓ Share the wealth.

In addition to the steps covered in this general discussion, oral history project managers will want to prepare for specific project considerations that can come up. Each of the points in the preceding checklist for legal/ethical considerations is a legal standards issue, but each also has an ethical component, as explained in the following discussion.

Share the information with the community. The ethical reminder in this consideration is based squarely on legal guidelines. Clarifying the legal status of interviews allows them to be shared by the community. Recognize the

> ### Important Legal Terms
>
> **Fair use** supports use of copyrighted works for teaching, scholarship, research, news reporting, criticism, and comment. It is determined by:
> - the purpose and character of the use, including whether it is for commercial or non-profit use,
> - the nature of the copyrighted work,
> - the amount of the copyrighted work used in proportion to the entire document, and
> - the effect of the use on the market for the copyrighted work or on its value.
>
> **Libel** is a published statement damaging to someone's reputation.
>
> **Slander** is a spoken statement damaging to someone's reputation.

importance to the community of clarifying ownership, of understanding what fair use is and its impact is on sharing information, and of identifying a partner or advisor to help with oral history preservation and access steps. The discussion about finding a repository in Chapter 6 is based on this consideration. Interviews should be cared for properly, and legal guidelines should be in place so interviews always are, or will be, accessible.[14]

Protect against slander and libel. When thinking about your community, it is easy to think about the great stories and detailed information an oral history project can generate. But what if someone describes a crime or says something potentially hurtful about someone else? This, again, is an oral history issue rooted in legal standards and ethical guidelines. Project directors can prepare for this possibility, although certainly hoping it will never occur, by reading the chapter on defamation in John Neuenschwander's *A Guide to Oral History and the Law*. Specifically review Sanford's Red Flag Words and include a discussion in your interview training about what interviewers should do if a questionable situation arises.[15] Project directors and team members should always remember that they are collecting history, not gossip, but they should not ignore difficult material if it adds substantive information to the historical record. Above all, if faced with a questionable legal circumstance in an interview, use your common sense. Follow a personal sense of ethics, clearly document a situation that makes anyone in the interview feel uncomfortable, and check with your legal advisor if you have a situation that needs resolving. Project directors also should understand that a Legal Release Agreement (Restrictions) may not hold up against a request made through the Freedom of Information Act or a subpoena.

Share the wealth. If you think your project might generate returns or income, discuss the situation as a team. There are several possibilities to consider; here are two of the most common. The first involves recording original performances of music or other artistic presentations. If this is a possibility for your project, seek guidance from legal advisors before you schedule an interview or turn on a recorder. You will want to negotiate what Mercier and Buckendorf describe in *Using Oral History in Community History Projects* as "reasonable remuneration."[16] Remuneration can vary from project to project; ask your advisors to help you develop a policy that will recognize the interviewees as creators of the original materials and include them in economic returns from project products that include their performances.

The second possibility involves quoting from oral history interviews in project products. This situation is very common; Legal Release Agreements, through transfer of copyright, provide access to interviews as primary source documents for this purpose. It again poses an ethical question, however. In general, researchers, guided by Principles and Best Practices of the Oral History Association, are reminded to use interview information accurately and in context. In addition, project directors will want to let interviewees know if a project includes a planned money-making product, such as a community or organizational fundraiser. In this case remuneration may take the form of public recognition at a community event and listing each interviewee's name in printed materials.

The time to think about how to handle this situation is before you begin recording interviews. You may find it helpful to develop a short project policy statement to cover this eventuality. The bottom line for sharing oral history wealth is straight-forward: anticipate situations, seek advice on how to handle them, and always recognize and respect each interviewee's gift of information to your community oral history project.

Managing Project Interviews

Managing interviews covers a variety of tasks, including making a final determination on the number of project interviews, choosing interviewees, and managing interviewees.

Determining the Number of Interviews

Determining the number of interviews to include in a project is another management decision. In their eagerness to document community history, project directors and teams can easily overshoot on this crucial figure. Before making a final decision, review the suggested interview number on the Project Design Statement and discuss the team's ability to meet it. Keep in mind that the standard for oral history is interviews that are both recorded and fully processed and that it takes approximately thirty hours per interview to meet this standard. Oral history consultants often can do a series of interviews, but volunteer interviewers generally do not complete more than one or two interviews a year.

It is quality, not quantity, that counts when deciding on the number of project interviews. **Volume 4,** *Interviewing in Community Oral History,* and **Volume 5,** *After the Interview in Community Oral History*, provide detailed information about interview and post-interview quality; review each carefully before making a numbers decision. As our Best Practices state, make it your goal to conduct interviews that stand the test of time. Make sure your project interviewers have time to prepare for interviews that go beyond the surface story and have the depth and nuance that truly reflect your community and its history. And, when the recorder is turned off, make sure responsibility for fully processing project interviews does not overload your team. Review the information on the Letter of Agreement for Repository, looking closely at the project tasks on this form, and reserve time to complete each of them. As part of full processing, include time to transcribe each interview, understanding it can take up to eight hours to transcribe one recorded hour.

 A project resulting in three to five oral history interviews can add up to 7.5 recorded hours and add 135 pages of new information to the historical record.

As you can see from the Project Design Statement in Chapter 2, the small community in the first fictitious oral history project, *Project One—Volunteer,* has a goal of three to five fully processed interviews. This may sound like a small number, but it is a manageable and realistic goal for a small project and it can generate a surprising amount of material. For example, at a standard length of 60 to 90 minutes per interview, the three to five interviews that team members will record will result in between 3 and 7.5 hours of interviews. Looking further to processing, with an average figure of 18 pages of transcript per recorded hour, the project will produce between 50 and 135 pages of accessible new information about the community's history to the historical record. That's the size of a book—and this is the smallest of our three fictitious projects. Using these figures, understand that your project, whatever its size, will make a noticeable contribution to the historical record of your community.

> "In your search to be inclusive, remember the person who appears to have no voice."
>
> *Mexican Voices, Michigan Lives (Part II), Diana Rivera, Chicano/Ethnic Studies Librarian, Michigan State University*

Interviewee Selection

Choosing the people to interview is a project director and team member responsibility.

A project plan should include a list of possible interviewees. Now is the time to review this list. Some of the choices will be obvious and thus easy. Other candidates, though they add only limited insight, may have never-before-documented information that should be included.

Use the project mission statement and the Interviewee Recommendation Form as guides when making interviewee choices. Begin by reviewing the information for each interviewee on the Interviewee Recommendation Forms and then ask yourselves the questions on the following checklist. Be inclusive and non-judgmental, and keep thorough notes about what you decide to do and why.

INTERVIEWEE SELECTION QUESTIONS

- ✓ How does information from each potential interviewee contribute to the project goals and mission statement?
- ✓ What impact would including each interviewee have on the project scope, focus, resources, and completion?
- ✓ Why have we included each interviewee in our project at this time and place to answer these questions asked by this interviewer?
- ✓ Have we included interviewees who represent all sides of the issues? If not, why not?
- ✓ Have any potential interviewees already been interviewed about our project topics and is that interview information available to our project? If so, is there a benefit to re-recording the information for our project? What is the best use of our resources?

When selecting an interviewee, ask yourself why this interviewee should be included in this project at this time and this place to talk about these topics.

If you have questions about interviewee choices, look again to your mission statement. Information from the Greenwich (CT) Library Oral History Project survey response shows us how this can work. The project, founded in 1973, is an on-going, volunteer-led project. Its mission statement, quoted in the *Toolkit's* planning volume, **Volume 2, *Planning a Community Oral History Project,*** identifies its purpose.

> *The Greenwich Library Oral History Project exists to collect, preserve, and make available the personal recollections of people who have helped to make or lived through and observed the history of Greenwich, Connecticut.*
>
> Greenwich (CT) Library Oral History Project,
> Catherine Ogden, Project Chair

Greenwich has many well-known residents, all of whom could be potential interviewee candidates. But Catherine Ogden, the project chair, understands high profile is not necessarily an interviewee choice criterion. This quote from Ogden's response to our survey explains what she means: "We have a clear mission statement. ... There are numerous well-known people living in town, but we do not interview them unless we can interview them *about* the town." Notice the emphasis in her response: as a project director, she understands and respects the direction the mission statement provides and uses it to guide management decisions regarding interviewee choices.[17]

Change in the Project Interviewee List

As discussed in **Volume 2, *Planning a Community Oral History Project,* Chapter 3,** the project interviewee list records the names and contact information of people identified as possible interviewees. Sometimes changes need to be made in the list. This can happen for a variety of reasons; be aware of the possibility and manage accordingly.

Answers to the following questions help maintain project focus while making necessary changes. After you've made a decision, document it in your project files and update the Project Design Statement.

QUESTIONS RELATING TO INTERVIEWEE LIST CHANGE AND UPDATES

✓ How would the addition of, or change in, interviewees affect project goals and purpose as defined by our mission statement?

✓ What impact would a change or addition have on our project scope, focus, and completion?

✓ Why would we decide to add these interviewees at this time and place to answer these questions asked by this interviewer? Why would we decide not to include these interviewees at this time and place?

✓ How would the addition of, or change in, interviewees affect our project resources? Do we have the resources to add or make these changes?

Recruiting Interviewees

Project directors sometimes consider using publicity to recruit project interviewees. Most oral history practitioners don't recommend this. While some projects may have success in publicly recruiting interviewees, generally, this encourages self-identification of an interviewee pool. An advertisement also implies the project will interview anyone who steps forward, which can counterbalance a careful selection of interviewees representing all sides of the interview topics. Use the mission statement, Interviewee Recommendation Form, and project research as guides when recruiting and selecting interviewees. Use public relations and advertising to tell people about what you are doing and to thank everyone involved in the project for their time and support.

Matching Interviewees with Interviewers

Matching interviewees and interviewers requires thought and care because the match can affect the interview outcome. Interviewer-interviewee assignments often involve same age, same sex and same ethnic background matches, although this does not have to be the case. People may be matched who know one another well or who have never met. The match should pair people who are compatible, can trust one another, and are willing to spend time together to do an interview. If you are matching people who know one another well, a common situation in community oral history projects, train the interviewers to watch for and deal with insider communication patterns. Keep thorough and detailed notes about interview assignment decisions. Document why and how interviewers and interviewees were matched and keep the notes with the project files.

Insider/Outsider Issues

Community oral history projects can face special challenges because interviewers and interviewees both may be seen as insiders with shared knowledge of the interview topics and an assumed understanding of the answers to questions. Ways to avoid the challenges typical of insider issues are presented in the following checklist.

INSIDER/OUTSIDER INTERVIEWING PRECAUTIONS

✓ Be aware of the need to solicit new or in-depth perspectives.
✓ Resist falling into a pattern of comparing experiences or memories.
✓ Remember to ask follow-up questions that further elicit interviewee information.

On the first point in the checklist, interviewers may not be willing or comfortable about asking for new information, especially if it counters standard community knowledge, and if asked, interviewees may be reluctant to answer. Regarding the second point, interviewers may fall into a familiar pattern of comparing information or stories rather than listening to the interviewee's stories. The third point describes another situation—failing to ask follow-up questions to clarify information because the nuances and meanings of a statement by an interviewee are shared by the interviewer.

Outsider issues most often stem from interviewers brought in to help with a project not taking the time to get to know the community or to fully understand what they are hearing in an interview. Rather than being accepted, they may be met by suspicion—not a good footing for an oral history interview.[18]

Each of these situations could easily come up in a community oral history project. Match your interviewers and interviewees carefully and discuss how to draw out as much detailed information as possible in an interviewer training workshop.

Interviewee Anonymity

Oral history project topics sometimes involve working with vulnerable interviewees. If this is the case, it may be necessary to protect their identities. Check with your legal resource advisors to determine what can and should be done if interviewee anonymity is needed.

Multi-Person Interviews

Oral historians usually interview one person at a time. One-on-one interviews support the kind of interaction between interviewer and interviewee that, ideally, results in communication of in-depth information in as open a way as possible from an interviewee's point of view.

Discussions about doing interviews with more than one person at a time often center on the possibility either of learning more about an event or way of life from a multi-person discussion or of learning more about a person or an event by observing personal interactions among interviewees. Although each possibility can result in interesting information, neither furthers the oral history goal of recording the specifics about an event or way of life from an interviewee's point of view. In fact, rather than the congenial give-and-take one might expect in such situations, multi-person interviews often end up either with one person dominating the discussion, with disagreements that bog down the interview or with someone not speaking up for fear of offending the others. Such situations can defeat the oral history standard of using interviews to record the voices of the voiceless. If you find your project will be doing multi-person interviews, review the precautions in the following checklist and think carefully about how to manage this process and teach interviewers to keep an interview moving along while drawing out everyone who is comfortable speaking in that setting.

MULTI-PERSON INTERVIEW PRECAUTIONS

✓ Voices sound alike on recordings. Ask a helper to take careful notes about who is speaking at all times, especially if the interview is audio-only.

✓ Ask each participant to say his or her name at the beginning of the interview to provide further speaker identification.

✓ If the interview will be audio-recorded only and a home video camera is available, run it just to identify speakers for the transcriber.

✓ Provide quiet members with an opportunity to speak, but if they want to remain quiet, respect their wishes.

As soon as possible after the interview, ask the interviewer and note taker to write up detailed notes about who was involved, what was said, who said it, and how each member of the group responded.

Scheduling Interviews

Scheduling an interview usually is an interviewer responsibility, but overseeing scheduling is a project management responsibility. Project directors will want to make sure interviews are scheduled and completed in a timely fashion. Use the Interview Summary and the Interview Tracking Form to keep track of interview progress.

Interviewer Training Workshop

Organizing and hosting an interviewer training workshop is another interview-related management responsibility. Interviewer training often takes a full day and should be mandatory, even for those who have previous community oral history experience. Training workshops present an opportunity not only to reinforce project interviewing standards but also to orient team members to the specifics of the project.

> "We held an all-day session with Geneva [Kebler Wiskemann] at which time she provided instruction on the oral interview process and helped in the development of a series of questions. … Prior to each interview, the interviewer and I developed a series of questions that were specified to the individual."
>
> *Leadership Interviews, Jewish Federation of Metropolitan Detroit (MI). Sharon Alterman, Director, Leonard N. Simons Jewish Community Archives, Jewish Federation of Metropolitan Detroit*

Sample Interviewer Training Workshop Agenda

- Workshop introductions
- Introduction to oral history and community oral history
- Introduction to the project and the orientation packet
- Ethical guidelines, including OHA *Principles* and *Best Practices* and our *Toolkit* Best Practices
- Legal standards, including use of the Legal Release Agreement
- Interview preparation and research
- Developing an interview question format
- Interviewing techniques
- Interviewer preparation, including insider-outsider issues
- Scheduling an interview and interview setting
- Note keeping, including providing a list of terms (controlled vocabulary basics)
- Running recording equipment—introduction and hands-on practice
- Record keeping, and filling out and using project forms
- Post-interview tasks
- Contact information for project director and work space access

Each workshop agenda item should cover the points critical to interview training; add any further items important for your project. The topic of recording equipment is an opportunity to present, or review, recording equipment training. Interviewer training covers a general list of interviewing "do's and don'ts"; the various presentations are often followed by discussion of specific project interviewing situations such as discussion of insider-outsider issues. Take time to thoroughly cover the interview setting, equipment placement, and interviewing techniques and include time to explain how to fill out and keep track of forms and other record-keeping materials, including signed Legal Release Agreements. You may find it helpful to assign an experienced mentor interviewer to a beginning interviewer as part of the interviewer training process and to schedule a feedback-and-discussion session after several project interviews have been completed.

Many project directors also develop a short interviewer training manual. If you decide to take this additional step, include project information, interviewing tips, and contact numbers and encourage interviewers to keep the manual handy as they do their interviews.

Sample Contents for an Interviewer Training Manual

- Oral history definition
- Project goals and mission statement
- Best Practices for Community Oral History Projects and copy of the Letter of Agreement for Interviewers
- Overview of ethical guidelines
- Overview of legal standards and copy of Legal Release Agreement
- Description of project recording equipment
- Copies of project forms
- Interviewing tips
- Checklist—after-the-interview responsibilities
- Project contact names and phone numbers

Figure 6.1. Interviewer training session, the Sound and Story Project Oral History Basics Workshop at the New Rochelle (NY) Public Library, 2011.
© Kristin Charles-Scaringi, Sound and Story Project

Repository

A repository, whether a library, historical organization, or other secure, long-term host, is the place to preserve all oral history project materials—files, master copies of interviews, a full set of transcripts, and original signed copies of Legal Release Agreements. Repositories hold collections of oral history project interviews, preserving them and making them accessible to others. This may sound straight-forward and easy, but it involves a complicated set of decisions and tasks.

The first step in this part of the interview management process is to find a repository that can accept project interviews and other materials and that has the resources to care for them and make them accessible to others. Not all repositories can or will do this. Many have restrictions about what they can accept; others, even if oral histories fall within their collecting areas, have staff and funding restrictions that may prevent their taking new projects. Review any recommendations your project planners have made and don't delay in following up on them.

Volume 2, *Planning a Community Oral History Project,* and **Volume 5,** *After the Interview in Community Oral History,* contain detailed information about contacting and working with repositories. Follow the guidelines in these volumes about what to look for in a repository, what to expect in discussions with repository personnel, and how to make an arrangement that benefits your project. Project directors should make this investigation a priority, regardless of how much time it takes. If needed, ask team members to help, and draw on community resource advisors for guidance and input.

 Don't assume you can always find a home for your project interviews; actively seek one out.

Once you've made a decision, to help the ensuing discussion run as smoothly as possible, negotiate an agreement with repository personnel, identifying who is responsible for what. Then, see that the negotiated points are written into a Letter of Agreement for Repository that both parties sign (see Figure 6.2).

As you can see, the Letter of Agreement for Repository identifies the repository and oral history project by name and provides a place for the signatures of representatives of both. Project scope is agreed on and stated in the form and bullet points describe the negotiated responsibilities of repository personnel and project team members.

Negotiate and put in place an agreement like this as early as possible. Doing this will allow you to incorporate legal, cataloging, and repository guidelines into your management decisions from the beginning of a project.

A secure, long-term web-hosted repository may be another possibility for providing basic long-term preservation and access to oral history project recordings. If so, look for one with as much disc space and bandwidth as you can find. Specifications, based on changing technology, will change rapidly. For the most up-to-date information, check with your state historical society or with the Oral History Association (www.oralhistory.org), or post a question on H-Oralhist, the oral history listserv (http://www.h-net.org/~oralhist/). Ask about the cost, policies for answering questions and resolving issues, and long-term care and migration policies and procedures.

 Do not substitute a project website for a long-term web-hosted repository.

LETTER OF AGREEMENT FOR REPOSITORY

This letter summarizes the responsibilities of the _Atlanta Public Library_ (repository) and the _Jazz Atlanta Oral History Project_ (oral history project). In addition to this document, a Legal Release Agreement form signed by each interviewer and interviewee will accompany each oral history.

The _Jazz Atlanta_ oral history project is responsible for the following tasks and for the costs incurred:

- Prepare audio- or video-recorded interviews in formats and quality determined by repository
- Transcribe oral history interviews according to style guidelines provided by repository
- Deliver signed Legal Release Agreement for each interview
- Deliver transcript and discs in format agreed upon.

The _Atlanta Public Library_ repository is responsible for the following tasks and for the costs incurred:

- Advise in selection and training of interviewers
- Advise in development of project plan
- Catalog oral histories for local catalog and WorldCat
- Format, copy, and bind oral history materials
- Make copies available for use according to repository's access policy.

Number of interviews _8–10_

Timeframe for delivery _2–2.5 years_

Number of copies of each interview _3_

REPOSITORY	ORAL HISTORY PROJECT
Name (print) _(insert name)_	**Name (print)** _Andrea Schmidt_
Signature _(sign here)_	**Signature** _(sign here)_
Title _Library Director_	**Title** _Project Director_
Date _(insert date)_	**Date** _(insert date)_

Figure 6.2. Sample—Letter of Agreement for Repository

As you think about your repository options, remember that the Internet, although it offers information access, is not set up to manage oral history projects. It provides a general service, but it does not offer or guarantee secure, long-term preservation of, and access to, anything posted on it.[19]

And, finally, a word of advice on interview management. Don't confuse managing interviews with doing the interviews. Each represents an area of responsibility. Interview management—the information covered in this chapter—is part of the oral history interview support system. These steps keep a project running smoothly, so project interviewers can collect and record a community's first-hand history in community oral history interviews.

CHAPTER 7

Winding Up

> **BEST PRACTICE NO. 2**
> Focus on oral history as a process.

> **BEST PRACTICE NO. 5**
> Make a plan.

> **BEST PRACTICE NO. 9**
> Process and archive all interview materials
> to preserve them for future use.

The purpose of this chapter is to look at after-the-interview steps from an oral history management point of view. We'll review managing interview preservation and access, storage and care, handling project files, and transcribing responsibilities. Finally, we'll review managing project public relations and project celebrations.

Oral history practitioners often hear about lost interviews—interviews that have become part of community lore but no longer can be found; the last anyone saw of them was when the data files didn't get transferred to a new computer and the external hard drive holding a copy was put in a shoebox on a closet shelf in a home now owned by someone else. Without a clear preservation plan, oral history recordings can be irretrievably lost within a relatively short period of time. A project director and team members will move on to other interests and, without meaning to, can lose or misplace the recordings. Fragile digital recordings also can deteriorate or be lost if they are not migrated to new technologies as they come along. The curatorial and technical details about how to preserve and maintain access to oral histories are discussed in **Volume 5**, *After the Interview in Community Oral History*; the management details related to preservation and access are covered here.

Preservation, for oral history management purposes, refers to actions taken to stabilize and protect the oral histories and the interview information they contain.

Access means the ability of repositories to make the interview information available and to locate it through finding aids, catalogs or websites.

> "The project was done in partnership with the Azusa City Library and the Friends of the Library. The library was the logical choice to anchor the project because it would archive, house and make the DVD and interview tapes/transcripts available to the community."
>
> *Azusa Heritage Project, Luisa Miranda and Arthur Ramirez, Project Director and Project Videographer/Cameraman*

Immediate Post-Interview Tasks

Oral history project management doesn't end when the recorder is turned off. Preservation and access begin with immediate post-interview management tasks. As soon as possible after the interview, begin to take care of each interview recording.

IMMEDIATE POST-INTERVIEW MANAGEMENT STEPS

- ✓ Make several copies of the interview recording in several formats and keep them in several places; label each with project name, interviewee name, and interview number from Interview Tracking Form.
- ✓ Maintain the original recording as the interview master copy; label it as Master Recording with the project name, interviewee name, and interview number from Interview Tracking Form.
- ✓ Complete all interview forms.
- ✓ Prepare to do the processing steps agreed on in Letter of Agreement for Repository.
- ✓ Keep the master recording and all materials related to each project interview in a central location in preparation for turning them over to a repository or other secure, long-term storage option.

Follow the LOCKSS principle for oral history digital recordings—Lots of Copies Keeps Stuff Safe.

Oral historians preserve recordings in widely available, cross-platform formats. Whether working with a repository or another secure, long-term storage option, choose and dedicate a computer with adequate storage space to preserve recordings and transcripts throughout the duration of the project. Then follow the LOCKSS principle—Lots of Copies Keeps Stuff Safe. This is one of the best preservation techniques. It is easy and cheap, and is something that every oral history project can do. Basically, it involves making multiple copies of each recording in multiple formats, on multiple media, and storing the copies in multiple physical locations—for instance, on a computer and one or more external hard drives. Label all copies with the same information, indicating one as the master copy. With this, you have completed the first after-the-interview tasks and are ready to move on to preservation management.

Managing Preservation

As for other areas of project management, managing preservation starts with steps identified on the management list in Chapter 1. The project director and team members are responsible for carrying out the processing steps agreed on in the Letter of Agreement for Repository. Processing, as done to the standards discussed in **Volume 5,** *After the Interview in Community Oral History,* includes:

- assigning team member responsibility for these processing steps,
- adding a metadata "envelope" that includes information about the interview, and
- developing written materials such as a recording abstract, interview log—also called interview index (optional)—and transcript.

Keep track of these steps on the Interview Tracking Form.

 Keeping project materials up-to-date and organized helps facilitate the preservation of interview information.

> **Important Preservation Management Terms**
>
> **Metadata** is the digital information describing an interview. It is packaged in an "envelope" which remains with the recording from the moment the recorder is turned off.
>
> A **recording abstract** is an interview summary. It includes the project name, names of the interviewer and interviewee, interview place and date, and content summary. Use the Interview Summary Form to develop a basic recording summary.
>
> An **interview log (index)** is an outline of the recorded interview. It lists the subject or subjects discussed at specific points in the interview from beginning to end. Consider skipping this step if you will be transcribing your interviews. You may want to replace it with a cumulative index to all project transcripts.
>
> A **transcript** is a verbatim (word-for-word) written copy of the interview. Transcribing removes the oral and visual communication but preserves the full interview content. If possible, use full transcription as a back-up and insurance against loss of information.

The project director is responsible for making sure these preservation management steps have been completed and all project oral histories are ready to be turned over to a repository or other secure, long-term storage. This includes using data on the Interview Summary and project files to provide basic information for cataloging and developing the written materials, including a transcript, that help preserve interview content. This work is time-consuming and detail-oriented; plan your time accordingly.

Long-Term Preservation Issues

One of the most commonly-asked questions about oral history preservation concerns the long-term status of interview recordings. Recordings can deteriorate, even in the best storage conditions and even if migrated to the highest technological standards. Or they can be put aside and forgotten or lost when preservation equipment is lost, sold, breaks down, or is replaced.[20]

Long-term oral history preservation management involves viewing interviews as two distinct forms.

- *Recordings.* These are audio and video representations of an interview, the actual primary source documents of oral history. Preserving oral history recordings provides access to full interview content, including voice inflections, visual representations if video is used, and other human insights. But recordings are fragile and digital materials present current and future preservation challenges.
- *Interview information.* This is the interview content—the information spoken by the interviewee on the recording. It is sometimes described as a translation of the primary source document from oral to written form. When preserved in written form with notations about voice inflections and human insights, but without the voice or visual, it represents basic interview information. A transcript is the standard format in which interview content is preserved; printed on acid-free paper and kept in an acid-free folder, it will last for years or centuries.

> "Our abstracts [summaries] are one-paragraph descriptions of the contents of each interview. The abstracts are used in four distinct ways:
>
> 1) The abstract appears at the beginning of each transcript to orient the user of the transcript to the contents of the interview.
>
> 2) The abstracts appear in the Special Collections section of our online archive. Each Special Collection online has an introduction to that collection along with an abstract for each interview to help people choose which interviews they want to listen to/read transcripts of. Each abstract links directly to the interview audio/transcript online.
>
> 3) The abstract appears in the Boulder Public Library's online catalog page for the interview.
>
> 4) The abstract appears as an interview description in our quarterly newsletter, which describes all of the interviews recently added to the collection and available to the public. This newsletter is available online and is 'Googleable,' so that the narrators and the abstract contents come up in a Google search."
>
> Susan Becker, *From Secrecy to Accessibility: The Rocky Flats (CO) Nuclear Weapons Plant Oral Histories*

Project directors and team members have a number of preservation options. Oral history practitioners, for example, sometimes opt for using recordings for shorter-term programmatic purposes, while using transcripts for long-term preservation of interview information. Weighing various possibilities and making decisions that serve long-term preservation needs within a project's and community's ability and resources to manage them is a responsibility not to be taken lightly.

> "We … store the audio tracks on the library servers. We also store all completed transcripts on the servers. We have a project to digitize all previous analog interviews, which is making good progress with four volunteers working on it when they can do so, and our ultimate goal is to convert all early typed transcripts to MS Word files and store them on the library's servers, as well. A new interview file folder on the servers has the audio track, all the interviewer's paperwork, the original verbatim transcript, the final transcript (with any changes made by the narrator), a title page, a credits page, and an index of the transcript."
>
> *Greenwich (CT) Library Oral History Project,*
> *Catherine (Cathy) H. Ogden, Chair*

Transcribing Overview

Transcribing is used by oral history practitioners to preserve and provide access to interview information. Oral history transcripts include footnotes, photographs, appendices and, in some cases, CVs, resumes, or other summaries of the interviewee's background. They also identify speech patterns and nonverbal communication in written form to help users understand what was in the original recording. The following checklist covers basic transcribing steps.[21]

TRANSCRIBING STEPS

- ✓ Obtain transcribing equipment—downloadable software for a computer plus a headset and foot pedal, or a machine made for transcribing purposes.
- ✓ Develop a transcribing guide specifying use of a standard, widely-available electronic format and including detailed style information.

- ✓ Ensure that the interview is transcribed word-for-word, taking care with spelling, including proper and place names, and that the punctuation documents the interview rhythm.
- ✓ Keep an electronic copy of each transcript on the project computer with the recording data file and another on an external hard drive or other form of external data storage.
- ✓ Print out the transcript on acid-free paper and keep the printed copy in an acid-free folder labeled with the project name, interviewee's name, and interview number from the Interview Tracking Sheet.

A look at these steps emphasizes the commitment it takes to develop project transcripts. But the advantages transcripts offer in preserving interview content far outweigh the time and effort it takes to produce them. In the following sidebar, Susan Becker, Program Manager of the Maria Rogers Oral History Project in Colorado, describes some of these benefits. Transcripts not only provide ease of use, they promote accuracy of use as well, clarifying words and phrases that may be difficult to decipher on a recording and providing correct spellings for proper names of people and places. As a result, they provide the user with a solid base from which to begin using interview information.

> "We produce transcripts of each interview for several reasons:
>
> 1) We have full audio online, but transcripts are easier for researchers to skim quickly. They then can go to the portion of the audio that is of interest.
>
> 2) Our online transcripts are word searchable, again making it easier for researchers to find exactly what they need.
>
> 3) It is easier for researchers to pull quotes (and we have more control over the accuracy of the quotes) if they are working from an audited transcript versus producing their own transcribed quotes.
>
> 4) When developing exhibits, documentaries, etc., it is much easier to develop a script or pull quotes from transcripts compared to starting from either video or audio files.
>
> In addition to the abstracts and transcripts, each of the interviews also is listed in the Boulder Public Library online catalog and can be accessed by keywords and Library of Congress Subject headings."
>
> *Susan Becker, From Secrecy to Accessibility: The Rocky Flats (CO) Nuclear Weapons Plant Oral Histories*

Figure 7.1. Veterans History Project Oral History Transcription in Progress, Douglas County History Research Center, Douglas County Libraries, Castle Rock, CO, 2007.

Transcriber Training Workshop

Project directors or designated team members should coordinate and oversee interview transcription, including organizing a transcriber training workshop.

> ### Sample transcriber training workshop agenda
>
> - Introductions
> - Introduction to oral history and community oral history
> - Introduction to the project (and project orientation packet)
> - Introduction to oral history transcribing
> - Introduction to transcribing equipment
> - Introduction to transcribing guide
> - Transcribing practice
> - Audit-editing practice
> - Wrap-up responsibilities

Workshops usually begin with introductions that cover the same content presented at an interviewer training workshop (see Chapter 6). Additional suggested agenda items are as follows:

- a discussion of project transcribing equipment,
- review of the transcribing guide and an introduction to project transcribing ethics and transcribing specifications,
- transcribing practice with the opportunity for hands-on equipment training using examples from project interviews,
- a review of audit-editing (accuracy checking) techniques, and
- information about where and how to ask questions and to turn in completed transcripts.

Transcriber training workshops usually are led by experienced transcribers. Project directors sometimes call on people with broad transcribing experience (medical transcribing, for example). If you are using this kind of resource, review the transcribing needs specific to your oral history project with the transcriber leading the workshop.

Plan on a two-to-three hour commitment for a transcriber training workshop. Give each workshop attendee a copy of the project transcribing guide, and make sure each attendee brings, or has available, equipment for the hands-on part of the agenda.

Sample Contents for a Project Transcribing Guide

- Introduction to project transcribing
- Oral history definition
- Project goals, mission statement, focus, and scope
- Best Practices for Community Oral History Projects and copy of Letter of Agreement for Transcribers
- Overview of ethical guidelines
- Description of project transcribing equipment
- Transcribing tips
- Word processing guide—format, font, type size, and line spacing, pagination specifications

(Continued on following page)

(continued)

- Cover page format
- Transcript page format, first page and inside page
- Footnote use guide
- Photo use guide
- Appendix or end material guide
- List of words common to the project
- Internet addresses for sites with standard oral history project transcribing guides, such as the Baylor Institute for Oral History Transcribing Guide
- Checklist for wrap-up responsibilities
- Project contact names and phone numbers

Managing Access

Access is an important part of the oral history definition included in the introduction to all *Toolkit* volumes. It provides the ongoing opportunity to share interview information with community members as well as all researchers and users.

Repository

If you are working with a repository, access to oral histories will be provided through the repository. If you will be looking for other options, you may end up being responsible for providing ongoing access to your project's oral histories. Here is a brief overview of access steps for project management purposes; for detailed guidelines and in-depth information about this issue, see **Volume 5,** *After the Interview in Community Oral History,* **Chapters 4 and 5.**

Oral histories are used in publications, exhibits, documentaries, plays, recordings, and websites. The possibilities are limited only by imagination. Access helps people find and make use of project interviews.

ACCESS GUIDELINES

✓ Use the Letter of Agreement for Repository as a guide for keeping in regular contact with the repository or secure, long-term storage option.

✓ Always make sure recordings are done, or can be provided, in a format that meets repository or secure, long-term storage management standards and guidelines.

✓ Catalog all materials and make them available through national and international cataloging systems.

Details for carrying out these broad guidelines vary. Some repositories only allow on-site access to interview information, while others provide full on-line access to recordings and transcripts. Most have the capacity to provide access to your oral history materials through their cataloging procedures, linking them to worldwide access resources. See **Volume 5,** *After the Interview in Community Oral History*, for detailed information on this subject.

Follow your project plan recommendations for desired level of access and work to manage this process. Vigilance in managing this step will pay off in maintaining access to the interview information.

Website

A website also is an excellent access tool. Websites are inviting and can communicate information about a community far beyond its defined boundaries, but they are not repositories, nor should they be. A project website is the place for a message that tells the world about a project and a community. Using copies of project interviews in formats that fit online specifications, project directors and team members often develop a website as a project product or outcome.

 Websites provide options for posting oral history interviews in a variety of formats.

Oral History Management Wrap-Up

As with any project, there always are final steps that need to be done. For oral history projects, these focus on interview disposition and budget review.

WRAP-UP STEPS

✓ Make sure all your project interview recordings are copied, stored as data files, fully processed, and accessible in recorded and transcribed formats.

✓ Make sure all your project and interview files are complete.
✓ Write a final project report summarizing your project results.
✓ Finalize the budget and close the project books.

Check off each item on the preceding list as you finish your project. And, as you do this, consider your public relations options.

> "Doing an oral history project … was full of many 'peaks and valleys.' I learned that it takes lots of dedication, passion, time and commitment and support to see it thru to completion, but the final product made all the work worth it!"
>
> *Azusa Heritage Project, Luisa Miranda and Arthur Ramirez, Project Director and Project Videographer/Cameraman*

Managing Public Relations

Public relations steps are helpful in communicating information about an oral history project to a community. Oral history practitioners develop and use public relations materials to keep communities informed about the project, its status, and its outcome. Articles in newspapers, newsletters, or online sites are good communication options. A project director may be asked to provide a speaker for a local historical society or library meeting or to discuss a project on a local radio call-in show. All of these outlets offer a forum to tell people about the project and its goals. And in doing so, they provide further opportunity to engage the community in the project.

I am including here, with permission, an example of an invitation to an exhibit developed as a project product using oral history project interview information (see Figure 7.2). It is part of the well-organized marketing or public relations strategy shown in the sidebar on page 136.

As you can see, the invitation to this traveling exhibit identifies the project, its community, the project director, institutions involved in its development, and its supporters. It also lists an active, yearlong exhibition schedule, providing information about when and where it was taking place. As a result, it helped spread information about the project and the community.

Your Story and Mine: A Community of Hope

You are invited to attend a multi-faceted, traveling exhibit created by formerly and currently homeless adults. This program will include a mural, individual works of art, photography, poetry and a short documentary video presenting an overview of homelessness.

Your Story and Mine: A Community of Hope uses the building blocks of history—personal oral traditions, artifacts, historic documents and family photographs—as literacy tools for those struggling with poverty, homelessness and a diminished sense of self. Advent House Ministries, in partnership with the Michigan Historical Museum in Lansing, Michigan, worked with homeless adults from a variety of cultural, ethnic and racial backgrounds to produce this exhibit with a generous grant from the Michigan Humanities Council. Adults enrolled in Advent House Ministries' GED and employment programs volunteered to participate in this project. Their stories reflect struggles with generational poverty and homelessness. All have faced and overcome a variety of personal obstacles in their efforts to gain stability and find permanent housing.

This exhibit will be touring the state of Michigan. Look for us at the following locations:

1. November 4, 2009: City Hall, Lansing
2. January, 2010: Capitol Area District Library, Lansing
3. February, 2010: Castle Museum of the Historical Society of Saginaw
4. March, 2010: Peter White Memorial Library, Marquette
5. April, 2010: Lansing area sites
6. May, 2010: Grand Rapids Public Library, Grand Rapids
7. June, 2010: Kalamazoo Public Library, Kalamazoo
8. July, 2010: To be determined
9. August, 2010: Traverse Area District Library, Traverse City
10. September, 2010: Manistique School and Public Library, Manistique

For information, contact: *(insert name)*

Figure 7.2. Publicity Statement. "Your Story and Mine: A Community of Hope," Lansing, MI. Source: Martha Aladjem Bloomfield, Project Director. Michigan Historical Museum, Community Relations Liaison, and Michigan Humanities Consultant.

> **MARKETING or PUBLIC RELATIONS STRATEGY**
> **Your Story and Mine: A Community of Hope**
>
> Advent House Ministries will work with all its partners to disseminate information about the project through a variety of media. Michigan Historical Museum and others will share mailing lists for media and organizations. Schools will be approached to use the panel exhibits as teaching tools for Michigan history. Advent House Ministries will acknowledge receipt of this grant and promote this project acknowledging the Michigan Humanities Council as the primary sponsor for the panel exhibit, the mural exhibit, DVD and Internet materials through its regular channels of press releases; email announcements; website materials, as well as publications and web sites of respective organizations where our traveling exhibits will reside. We will seek interviews with newspapers and radio and television programs in communities where the exhibits will be on display.
>
> Source: Martha Aladjem Bloomfield, Project Director. Michigan Historical Museum, Community Relations Liaison, and Michigan Humanities Consultant.

Celebration

A number of years ago (1983), a group of Minnesota interviewers developed an oral history project about the Civilian Conservation Corps (CCC) in the state. The project resulted not only in interviews but also in development of an archival collection containing thousands of photographs and scrapbooks; hundreds of copies of camp newsletters and other materials; and an artifacts collection containing tools, uniforms, CCC-issued trunks, and other items. As the project came to an end, the project director and team members decided to hold a celebration. They reserved time in the museum and archive serving as the project repository, ordered in cookies and juice, and sent out invitations. Attendance at the celebration set a record for one-day attendance that has not yet been broken at that institution. This was due in part to the pride attendees and their families felt about being in the CCC. It also illustrated the pride they felt in knowing their stories were documented for their community and preserved for future generations.

Another project recently reported a similar experience. In a response on a community oral history survey, the In Our Own Words, The Negro Spirituals Heritage Keepers project described the "overwhelmingly large crowd that turned out" for their public celebration. As discussed earlier, oral history projects attract interest and attention in a community. Celebrations are a way to capture this interest and bring attention to the project and the community.[22]

Use your celebration to thank interviewees for their stories, interviewers and other team members for their participation in the project, and supporters for everything they did for the project. Also, don't forget to thank your project director; the director's willingness to provide steady project guidance and to see the project through deserves an extra round of applause.

> "Occasionally we stage special events, such as book parties. We have celebrated our five-year anniversaries with Oral History Day since our thirtieth year (on our 25th anniversary our office was under construction). On Oral History Day, we invite the public to sign up for half-hour interviews on any topic they wish; in 2008, we suggested World War II home front interviews. Both events (2003, 2008) were extremely successful. In 1986 community members produced a successful musical revue based on the OHP's interviews, 'We've Been Here All Along.'"
>
> *Greenwich (CT) Library Oral History Project,*
> *Catherine (Cathy) H. Ogden, Chair*

Congratulations to community oral historians on projects well managed and jobs well done.

APPENDIX

Management Survey and Respondents

ORAL HISTORY PROJECT MANAGEMENT SURVEY
Community Oral History Toolkit

Please return by February 25, 2011

In 2009, some of you participated in a project planning survey for an oral history toolkit by Nancy MacKay, Mary Kay Quinlan, and Barbara W. Sommer under contract with Left Coast Press, Inc. We want to thank you for participating in that survey. We have drawn on your planning survey responses for the project planning volume.

Now we have another set of questions. After project planning is completed, the next step is project management. We'd like to hear how you manage the nuts and bolts of your oral history project on a day-to-day basis, so we've developed a follow-up to our planning survey. It has the same format as the planning survey but covers project management steps. Will you fill it out and <u>return it to Barb Sommer by February 25, 2011?</u> *Your responses will help us as we develop the project management volume in our toolkit series.*

PROJECT OVERVIEW

Project Name:

Project Topic:

Primary Goal

❑ Collect oral histories

❑ Support exhibit development
   Exhibit title:

❑ Part of a festival or celebration
   Name of event:

❑ Community building

❑ Other—Describe:

Would you say your project has met or is meeting your primary goal?

❑ Yes   ❑ No

Please explain:

Did your project add goals during the interviewing period?

❑ Yes   ❑ No

Please explain:

Additional comments:

Number of interviews:
   _____ Scheduled
   _____ Completed

Is interviewing on track with your projected timeline?

❑ Yes   ❑ No

Please explain:

Additional comments:

Project Work Timeline

Dates:

❑ Has your project work timeline remained the same?

❑ Changed? Please explain:

Additional comments:

Repository

Name:
Oral histories available through (check all that apply)
❑ library
❑ archive
❑ digital repository (Note: this does not include posting interviews online)
❑ other

Describe how you manage contacts with your *repository*:

Funding

List your project funding sources.

Has your project funding met projections?   ❑ Yes   ❑ No
Please explain:

Additional comments:

Project Management Style

How would you describe your project management style?

Describe what is most important about your project management style to you and to your project.

Summary—Project Management Steps

1. How would you rate the importance of each of the following oral history project management steps?

   Rate on a scale of 1-5, with 1 low and 5 high.
   Add comments on this sheet or use another sheet.

Management Step	Importance of step	Comments	Other (describe)
Use project name in project materials			
Use purpose/mission statement as a guide to project management			
Maintain project work timeline			
Complete projected number of interviews			
Keep volunteers or workers familiar with the project involved in it			
Maintain interviewer training standards			
Maintain contacts with repository			
Use project management forms including legal release form			
Review and maintain budget, track expenses			
Review and maintain grants, submit final reports			
Maintain recording equipment			
Maintain recording media			
Process interviews			
Continue funding outreach			
Use publicity plan			

2. Identify management responsibilities. Check all that apply. Use separate sheet to describe consultant duties as needed. If the Project Director and Interviewer are the same person, check here_____.

Management Step	Project Director	Project Interviewer(s)	Project helpers	Project Treasurer	Consultant (describe)
Use project name in project materials					
Keep project focused on purpose/mission statement					
Keep focused on projected work timeline					
Do planned number of interviews					
Add interviews (if needed)					
Keep volunteers or workers familiar with project and involved in it					
Maintain interviewer training					
Oversee interview contacts and interviewing process					
Maintain contacts with repository					
Use project management forms including legal release form					
Review and maintain budget, track expenses					
Review and maintain grants, submit final reports					
Use and maintain recording equipment					
Use and maintain recording media					
Process interviews					
Continue funding outreach					
Use publicity plan					

3. Did you use management steps not listed on the above tables? If so, list and comment.

4. Narrative Questions (use extra space as needed, bullet-point summaries are fine)

   4.1   Describe your project.

   4.2   Describe project management process and critical project decisions.

   4.3   Which of the oral history project management steps listed on the above tables did you find most helpful and why?

   4.4   Which of the oral history project management steps listed on the above tables did you find least helpful and why?

   4.5   Describe working with your donor (legal release) form including where and how it was developed, copyright language used, and questions about its use.

4.6 Describe your project management equipment and media decisions.

4.7a Describe your project budget projections including budget categories. Identify the most costly item in your budget and why. It is not necessary to include itemized budget figures, but it will be helpful to know your total budget range:

❏ less than $1,000   ❏ $1,000-$5,000   ❏ $5,001-$10,000

❏ $10,001-$25,000   ❏ $25,001-$100,000

❏ over $100,000 (amount if you wish to indicate _____)

4.7b Describe your actual project budget including budget categories. Identify the most costly item in your budget and why. It is not necessary to include itemized budget figures, but it will be helpful to know your total budget range:

❏ less than $1,000   ❏ $1,000-$5,000   ❏ $5,001-$10,000

❏ $10,001-$25,000   ❏ $25,001-$100,000

❏ over $100,000 (amount if you wish to indicate _____)

4.8 Describe managing your project funding sources.

4.9a Describe managing donation of project interview materials to a repository.

4.9b Describe managing donations of photographs, archival materials and other interview-related items.

4.10a What processing techniques did you use and why?

❏ abstract   ❏ transcript   ❏ abstract and transcript

4.10b When did you begin processing your project materials and why?

4.11 Looking back, what would you say are one or two management highlights about the project and why?

4.12 Is there anything more you would like to tell us about project management? Add your thoughts and comments.

5. Oral History Project Examples. Attach as many as you wish.
    - ❑ Project Name
    - ❑ Project Mission Statement
    - ❑ Donor (Legal Release)
    - ❑ Project Budget indicating itemized categories
    - ❑ Abstract
    - ❑ Transcript Excerpt
    - ❑ Agenda—Interviewer Training Session
    - ❑ Publicity Plan
    - ❑ Other (identify)

Survey Responder(s):

Organization/Position(s):

    Address:

    Telephone:

    Email:

    Website:

PLEASE RETURN BY February 25, 2011

email to barbsom@aol.com

THANK YOU VERY MUCH FROM ALL OF US. WE'LL KEEP YOU POSTED ON OUR PROJECT.

Thank you to the responders to the oral history project planning and management surveys.

The Azusa Heritage Project, Azusa, CA. Luisa Miranda, Project Director, and Arthur Ramirez, Videographer/cameraman.

Bland County History Archives/Place-Based Education, Rocky Gap, VA. John Dodson, Director of the Bland County History Archives and the Mountain Home Center.

Chippewa Valley Museum, Eau Claire, WI. Susan McLeod, Director.

Dana Point Historical Society Oral History Project, Dana Point, CA. Mary A. Crowl, Director.

El Toro Marine Corps Air Station Oral History Project, Fullerton, CA. Janet Tanner, California State University, Fullerton, Center for Oral and Public History.

The Freight & Salvage: An Oral History, Berkeley, CA. Andrea Hirsig, House Manager, Freight & Salvage Coffee House.

Greenwich Library Oral History Project, Greenwich, CT. Catherine H. (Cathy) Ogden, Chairman.

Immigration History Research Center (MN). Elizabeth Haven Hawley, Program Director, Immigration History Research Center, University of Minnesota, Twin Cities.

In Our Own Words, The Negro Spirituals Heritage Keepers, Oakland, CA, Sam Edwards and Lyvonne Chrisman, co-founders, Friends of the Negro Spirituals.

Iron Range Research Center, Chisholm, MN. Scott Kuzma, Director.

Leadership Interviews, Jewish Federation of Metropolitan Detroit, Bloomfield Hills, MI. Sharon Alterman, Director, and Leonard N. Simons Jewish Community Archives, Jewish Federation of Metropolitan Detroit

Mackinac Bridge Oral History Project, Lansing, MI. Michigan Oral History Association, Geneva Kebler Wiskemann, Founder/Secretary.

Marquette General Health Services, Marquette, MI. Russell M. Magnaghi, Project Director and Interviewer, Northern Michigan University, Director, Center for Upper Peninsula Studies.

Meaningful Stories, Meaningful Lives, JARC, Farmington Hills, MI. Karen Siersma Rosenstein, Judaic Services Coordinator.

Mexican Voices, Michigan Lives - Part II (I), East Lansing, MI. Diana Rivera, Chicano/Ethnic Studies Librarian, Michigan State University.

"Your Story and Mine: A Community of Hope," Lansing, MI. Martha Aladjem Bloomfield, Project Director, Michigan Historical Museum, Community Relations Liaison, and Michigan Humanities Consultant.

Oakland Chinatown Oral History Project, Oakland, CA. Angela Zusman, Project Manager, Phase 1.

"From Secrecy to Accessibility: The Rocky Flats Nuclear Weapons Plant Oral Histories," Boulder, CO. Susan Becker, Maria Rogers Oral History Program Manager; Cyns Nelson, Voice Preserve: Oral historian, archivist; LeRoy Moore, Rocky Mountain Peace and Justice Center; Hannah Nordhaus, oral historian, journalist.

Savannah Jewish Archives Oral Histories, Savannah, GA. Lynette Stoudt, Archivist, Savannah Jewish Archives (Senior Archivist, Georgia Historical Society); Kaye Kole, Project Director.

Smith College Club of Minnesota, Oral History Project, Eden Prairie, MN. Betsey Whitbeck, Smith College Club of Minnesota, President.

Surfing Heritage Foundation Oral History Committee, San Clemente, CA. Paul Holmes, Surfing Heritage Foundation Oral History Committee Chair.

Worcester Women's History Project, Oral History Initiative, Worcester, MA. Lisa Krissoff Boehm, Professor of Urban Studies, Project Consultant.

NOTES

1. See also Laurie Mercier and Madeline Buckendorf, *Using Oral History in Community History Projects,* the Oral History Association, 2007.

2. For additional information about the oral history process, see David K. Dunaway and Willa K. Baum. *Oral History: An Interdisciplinary Anthology,* 2nd ed. (Walnut Creek, CA: AltaMira Press, 1996); Nancy MacKay, *Curating Oral Histories: From Interview to Archive* (Walnut Creek, Left Coast Press, Inc., 2007); Robert Perks and Alistair Thomson, *The Oral History Reader,* 2nd ed. (New York: Routledge, 2006); Donald A. Ritchie, *Doing Oral History: A Practical Guide,* 2nd ed. (New York: Oxford University Press, 2003); Donald A. Ritchie, *The Oxford Handbook of Doing Oral History* (New York: Oxford University Press, 2010); Barbara W. Sommer and Mary Kay Quinlan, *The Oral History Manual,* 2nd ed. (Lanham, MD: AltaMira Press, 2009); Valerie Raleigh Yow, *Recording Oral History: A Guide for the Humanities and Social Sciences,* 2nd ed. (Walnut Creek, CA: AltaMira Press, 2005).

3. Questionnaire for Community Oral History Projects, Mackinac Bridge Oral History Project, Lansing, MI. Michigan Oral History Association, Geneva Kebler Wiskemann, Founder/Secretary.

4. For further reading, see: Alexander Freund, "Oral History as Process-Generated Data," http://blog.uwinnipeg.ca/alexander-freund/2009/08/oral_history_as_processgenerat.html, accessed September 1, 2009; Linda Shopes, "What Is Oral History?" http://historymatters.gmu.edu/mse/oral/oral.pdf, accessed May 21, 2012.

5. "Principles and Best Practices," Oral History Association, http://www.oralhistory.org/about/principles-and-practices/, accessed October 10, 2012.

6. For more information, see: John A. Neuenschwander, *A Guide to Oral History and the* Law (New York: Oxford University Press, 2009) and *Oral History and the Law,* 3rd, ed., John Neuenschwander for the Oral History Association, 2002.

7. Barbara W. Sommer and Mary Kay Quinlan, *The Oral History Manual*, 2nd ed. (Lanham, MD: AltaMira Press, 2009):69-70.
8. Catherine H. Ogden, Chair. Greenwich (CT) Library Oral History Project Management Survey Response, 2011.
9. "Boyd describes efforts to develop best digital practices for oral history" in the *Oral History Association Newsletter*, Winter 2011: volume XIV, number 3:6.
10. Barbara W. Sommer and Mary Kay Quinlan, *The Oral History Manual*, 2nd ed. (Lanham, MD: AltaMira Press, 2009):55-56.
11. Oral History Project Management Survey: Community Oral History Project. The Immigration History Research Center (MN), Elizabeth Haven Hawley, Program Director, 2011.
12. For an example of websites that compile information about national grants opportunities, see the Council on Library and Information Resources and its "Cataloging Hidden Special Collections and Archives" page, http://www.clir.org/awards/HC_Related_Programs.html, accessed February 1, 2012.
13. John Neuenschwander, *A Guide to Oral History and the Law* (New York: Oxford University Press, 2009).
14. For a detailed discussion of legal issues regarding uses of oral histories, see John A. Neuenschwander, *A Guide to Oral History and the* Law (New York, Oxford University Press, 2009):72-82. Although copyright does not need to be filed for copyright protection of oral histories, it must be registered before an infringement lawsuit can be filed.
15. John A. Neuenschwander, *A Guide to Oral History and the* Law (New York, Oxford University Press, 2009):31-47. See Table 4.1 for a list of Sanford's Red Flag Words. See also: John Neuenschwander, "What's in your legal release agreement?" in the *Oral History Association Newsletter*, Fall 2007, Volume XLI, Number 2:3,7,8.
16. For further discussion, see Laurie Mercier and Madeline Buckendorf, *Using Oral History in Community History Projects*, the Oral History Association, 2007:32-34 and Barbara W. Sommer and Mary Kay Quinlan, *The Oral History Manual*, 2nd ed. (Lanham, MD: AltaMira Press, 2009):28-29.
17. Oral History Project Management Survey: Community Oral History Project. Greenwich Library Oral History Project (OHP), Greenwich, CT. Catherine (Cathy) H. Ogden, Chairman, 2011.
18. See Laurie Mercier and Madeline Buckendorf, *Using Oral History in Community History Projects*, the Oral History Association, 2007:28-30. See also Barbara W. Sommer and Mary Kay Quinlan, *The Oral History Manual*, 2nd ed. (Lanham, MD: AltaMira Press, 2009):63-65 for an example of cross-cultural interviewing issues that may be helpful when discussing insider-outsider questions.
19. For additional discussion on this topic, see the Oral History Association LinkedIn message thread, June 2012.

20. See "When Data Disappears" by Kari Krause in *The New York Times,* Sunday Review: The Opinion Pages, August 6, 2011, for a discussion of this topic.
21. For examples of transcription guides, see Baylor Institute for Oral History Transcribing Guide (http://www.baylor.edu/oralhistory/index.php?id=23607); Transcribing, Editing and Processing Guidelines of the Minnesota Historical Society (http://www.mnhs.org/collections/oralhistory/ohtranscribing.pdf).
22. Response to "Questionnaire for Community Oral History Projects" from In Our Own Words, The Negro Spirituals Heritage Keepers, Sam Edwards and Lyvonne Chrisman, co founders, Friends of the Negro Spirituals, 2009.

FURTHER READING

Books

MacKay, Nancy. *Curating Oral Histories: From Interview to Archive.* Walnut Creek, CA: Left Coast Press, Inc. 2007.

Neuenschwander, John A. *A Guide to Oral History and the Law.* New York, Oxford University Press, 20090.

Ritchie, Donald A. *Doing Oral History: A Practical Guide,* 2nd ed. New York: Oxford University Press, 2003.

Sommer, Barbara W. and Mary Kay Quinlan. *The Oral History Manual,* 2nd ed. Lanham, MD: AltaMira Press, 2009.

Trimble, Charles E., Barbara W. Sommer, and Mary Kay Quinlan. The American Indian Oral History Manual: Making Many Voices Heard. Walnut Creek, CA: Left Coast Press, Inc., 2008.

Pamphlets

Mercier, Laurie, and Madeline Buckendorf. *Using Oral History in Community History Projects,* for the Oral History Association, 2007.

Neuenschwander, John A. *Oral History and the Law,* 3rd ed., for the Oral History Association, 2002.

Articles

Boyd, Doug. "Preserving the Past," presentation at Oral History Preservation 101 Workshop, Kentucky Oral History Commission, Kentucky Historical Society, June 3, 2008.

Henson, Pamela. "From Analog to Digital: The Smithsonian Institution Archives Digital Preservation Initiative" in *The Oral History Association Newsletter,* Winter 2009:XLIII:3.

Preserving State Government Digital Information: Digital Audio and Video White Paper, unpublished paper, Minnesota Historical Society, May 2009.

"Boyd describes efforts to develop best digital practices for oral history" in the *Oral History Association Newsletter,* Winter 2011:XLV:3.

Websites

Capturing the Living Past: An Oral History Primer. An oral history tutorial on the Nebraska State Historical Society website, http://www.nebraskahistory.org/lib-arch/research/audiovis/oral_history/index.htm, accessed January 26, 2012.

Federal Agencies Digitization Guidelines Initiative AV Working Group, http://www.digitizationguidelines.gov/audio-visual, accessed November 29, 2010.

Freund, Alexander. "Oral History as Process-Generated Data," http://blog.uwinnipeg.ca/alexander-freund/2009/08/oral_history_as_processgenerat.html, accessed September 1, 2009.

Library of Congress Packard Campus for Audio-Visual Conservation, http://www.loc.gov/avconservation/packard/, accessed June 7, 2012

Making Sense of Oral History. History Matters: The U.S. Survey Course on the Web, http://historymatters.gmu.edu/mse/oral, accessed December 13, 2011.

Minnesota Historical and Cultural Grants Manual: Oral History, Minnesota Historical Society Local History, http://www.mnhs.org/legacy/grants/manual/oral_history.htm, accessed May 10, 2012.

Minnesota Historical Society Oral History Collection. The Minnesota Historical Society, http://www.mnhs.org/collections/oralhistory/oralhistory.htm, accessed February 28, 2012.

Oral History in the Digital Age (OHDA) guidelines, http://ohda.matrix.msu.edu, accessed September 15, 2012.

Oral History, Digital Oral History Workshop, Digital Video Recording, Baylor Institute for Oral History, http://www.baylor.edu/content/services/document.php/79770.pdf, accessed February 9, 2012.

Oral History/Oral History Workshop for Students (Parts 1-4 and Quiz), Baylor Institute for Oral History, http://www.baylor.edu/oral_history/index.php?id=56194, accessed June 12, 2010.

Oral History/Oral History Workshop for Teachers (Parts I-IV and Quiz), Baylor Institute for Oral History, http://www.baylor.edu/oral_history/index.php?id=56907, accessed June 10, 2010.

"Preserving State Government Digital Information," Bibliographic Center for Research Collaborative Digitization Program's (CDP) Best Practices Digital Imaging Working Group, "BCR's Digital Imaging Best Practices," Version 2.0, June 2008, http://www.bcr.org/dps/cdp/best/digital-imaging-bp.pdf, accessed December 28, 2009.

"Style Guide for Transcribing Oral History," Institute for Oral History at Baylor University, http://www3.baylor.edu/Oral_History/Styleguiderev.htm, accessed November 19, 2007.

"Transcribing, Editing, and Processing Guidelines," Minnesota Historical Society, http://www.mnhs.org/collections/oralhistory/ohtranscribing.pdf, accessed November 19, 2007.

Organizations

Oral History Association. Organization of oral history practitioners. www.oralhistory.org

The Consortium of Oral History Educators. AOHELanman@aol.com

Oral History Listserv. H-Oralhist is an international network for scholars and professionals active in studies related to oral history: http://www.h-net.org./~oralhist/

INDEX

A

abstracts of interviews, 127
academia, projects originating in, 10
access
    confidentiality issues and, 79
    data preservation kit to ensure, 87
    defining, 124
    to equipment storage space, 65
    managing, 132–33
    repositories and, 132, 133
accountants, 54
acknowledgements, 64
Advent House Ministries project in Michigan, 135–36
after-the-interview tasks. *See* post-interview tasks
archives, 13, 85
Arrowhead Civilian Conservation Corps Documentation Project, 136
audits, as grant requirement, 97

B

bartering, obtaining donations by, 98
Becker, Susan, 129
Best Practices (OHA), 42
best practices, overview of, 12–13
bookkeepers, 54
books as possible outcomes, 28
Boyd, Douglas, 87
Buckendorf, Madeline, 110

budget
    expense categories, 99–100
    project director responsibilities, 49, 102–3
    records management, 49
    sample, 100–102
    wrap-up steps, 134
businesses, donations from local, 98

C

Carmel-by-the-Sea (California) Voices Oral History Project. *See* volunteer fictitious project
catalogers (trained), 54–55
celebrations, 136–37
city fictitious project
    budget, 103
    Interviewee Biographical Profile, 70
    Interviewee Recommendation Form, 69
    Interview Summary, 73–74
    Interview Tracking Form, 75–76
    Legal Release Agreement, 44–45
    Letter of Agreement for Interviewer, 60
    Letter of Agreement for Repository, 121
    management notes, 34
    overview of, 20, 21, 34
    Photograph and Memorabilia

160 | Index

Receipt, 77–78
Project Design Statement, 35–37
team members, 66–67
Team Member Time Sheet, 62
work space, 67
Civilian Conservation Corps (CCC), Minnesota project, 136
colleges, bartering with, 98
committees, role of, 18
community
  defining, 10, 20
  documenting contributions from supporters, 99
  inclusion of all members, 12
  management of supporters, 48, 63
  public relations and, 134
  representing project to, 48
  role during management phase, 24, 25
  sharing interviews with, 108–9
  sharing success with, 13
community oral history, defining, 20
community oral history projects
  best practices, 12–13
  defining, 10, 20
  differences with academic projects, 10
confidentiality issues, 79, 108
consistency
  commitment to project duration by team members, 48, 55
  importance of, 49
consultants
  roles of, 28, 55
  typical number of interviews by, 111
copyright, 42
Cushman Motor Works Project in Lincoln, Nebraska, 27–28

D
data files, preservation of, 84–85, 87
documentation
  of changes, 113
  of contributions from community supporters, 99
  of dollar value of volunteers, 67
  management of forms, 68
  See also files; sample forms

donations
  on sample budget, 100–101
  tips for acquiring, 98
  value of, 97
duration. *See* time

E
envelope, for packaging metadata, 125, 126
ethical considerations
  for interview management, 108–10
  OHA guidelines, 42
  overview of, 12
expenses, 99–101
external microphones, advantages of, 84, 86

F
fair use, described, 109
fictitious oral history project examples. *See* city fictitious project; historical society fictitious project; volunteer fictitious project
files
  confidentiality and access, 79
  importance of, 78, 80
  storage and maintenance of data, 84–85
  suggested materials for interviewee, 79
  suggested materials for project, 78–79
fiscal sponsors/agents, described, 94
forms
  for funds management, 97
  as management tools, 68
  for recording equipment kit, 86
  reviewing and managing, 49
  See also sample forms
Freedom of Information Act requests, 110
From Secrecy to Accessibility: The Rocky Flats Cold War Museum Plant Oral Histories in boulder Colorado, 129
funders role during management phase, 24, 25
funding
  defining, 92
  documentation requirements, 67, 97
  donations, 97–98

sources of, 92–93
See also grants

G
General Principles (OHA), 42
goals
    grant requirements and, 97
    historical focus and, 106
    refining during management, 28
grants
    national sources of, 93
    requirements, 67, 94, 97
    on sample budget, 100–101
    writing, 27, 94–97
Greenwich, Connecticut Library Oral History Project, 63, 113
Guide to Oral History and the Law, A (Neuenschwander), 109

H
Hawley, Elizabeth Haven, 91
historical context, importance of, 107
historical focus
    dealing with new topics, 107
    importance of, 106
    overview of, 29
    reviewing, 106–7
historical societies, 21, 27
historical society fictitious project
    budget, 103
    management notes, 38
    overview of, 20, 21, 38
    Project Design Statement, 39–41
    team members, 67
    work space, 67
H-Oralhist listserv, 120
humanities councils, as resource, 93

I
income, 100–102, 110
index to interviews, 126
in-kind donations, 67
In Our Own Words project, 137
In Our Own Words: The Negro Spirituals Heritage Keepers Project (Friends of Negro Spirituals), 137
insider/outsider issues, 114–15
Institute of Museum and Library Services (IMLS), 93

Internet, 122, 127
interns, 55
Interviewee Biographical Profile Form, 70–72
Interviewee Recommendation Form, 68–69
interviewees
    anonymity of, 115
    changes in list of, 113–14
    importance of inclusivity, 112
    matching with interviewers, 114
    recruiting, 114
    remuneration for, 110
    selecting, 112–13
    suggested materials for files, 79
interviewers
    description of responsibilities, 57–58
    Letter of Agreement sample, 60
    matching with interviewees, 114
    preparation time for interviews, 111
    recording equipment training workshops, 88–90
    responsibilities, 52
    skills needed, 52–53
    training, 13, 50, 117–18
    as transcribers, 53
    using mentors, 118
interview log/index, described, 126
interviews
    abstracts of, 127
    average time to complete each, 50, 111
    community and content, 24, 25
    containing performances, 110
    determining number of, 111–12
    ethical/legal management considerations, 108–10
    funders and content, 24, 25
    importance of groundwork, 13
    importance of historical context, 107
    Letter of Agreement for Repository processing requirements for, 111, 125
    lost, 123
    management support of, 24–25
    multi-person, 115–16
    preparation time for, 111

preservation of, 13, 127
recorded hours for each, 111
reviewing specific subjects/themes to cover, 106–7
scheduling, 116
sharing with community, 108–9
space needs for, 65
use of quotations from, 110
wrap-up steps, 133–34
See also entries beginning with *transcri*
Interview Summary
about, 72
sample, 73–74
used for recording abstract, 126
Interview Tracking Form, 74–76
iPhones as recording equipment, 84
It Takes a Village to Make a City: Duluth (MN) Residents Speak Out Oral History Project. *See* historical society fictitious project

J
Jazz Atlanta Oral History Project. *See* city fictitious project

L
legal considerations
copyright, 42
for interview management, 108–10
Legal Release Agreement, 42–43
Legal Release Agreement (Restrictions), 43, 45–46
need for legal expert on team, 55
overview of, 12
terms, 109
Legal Release Agreement
management notes, 42–43
responsibilities of project director, 108
sample, 44
Legal Release Agreement (Restrictions)
about, 43
legal strength of, 110
management notes, 46
sample, 45
Letter of Agreement for Interviewer
about, 59, 64

management notes, 59
sample, 60
Letter of Agreement for Repository
about, 120
processing requirements of, 111, 125
sample, 121
Letter of Agreement for Transcriber
about, 59, 64
management notes, 59
sample, 61
libel, 109
libraries, 54, 98, 124
Library Oral History Project in Greenwich, Connecticut, 63, 113
Lincoln, Nebraska, Cushman Motor Works project, 27–28
listserv, H-Oralhist, 120
loans, sources of non-monetary, 98
LOCKSS principle, 125

M
management
guide for, 29
overview of steps, 22–25
survey, respondents to, 148–49
survey sample, 139–47
management notes
for city fictitious project, 34
for historical society fictitious project, 38
for Interviewee Biographical Profile Form, 70
for Interviewee Recommendation Form, 68
for Interview Summary, 72–73
for Interview Tracking Form, 75
for Legal Release Agreement, 42–43
for Legal Release Agreement (Restrictions), 46
for Letter of Agreement for Interviewer, 59
for Letter of Agreement for Transcriber, 59
for Photograph and Memorabilia Receipt, 76–77
for volunteer fictitious project, 30
Maria Rogers Oral History Project, 129
McLeod, Susan, 105
media, described, 86

mentor interviewers, 118
Mercier, Laurie, 110
metadata, described, 125, 126
Michigan Advent House Ministries project, 135–36
microphones, advantages of external, 84, 86
Minnesota Civilian Conservation Corps Documentation Project, 136
Minnesota Historical and Cultural Grants Manual oral history guidelines, 94–96
mission statement
   grant requirements and, 97
   as guide for choosing interviewees, 113
   historical focus and, 106
   maintaining focus on, 49
   overview of, 28
   reviewing, 107
   team recruitment and, 55
monetary sources. *See* funding
multi-person interviews, 115–16

N
name, overview of, 28
National Endowment for the Arts (NEA), 93
National Endowment for the Humanities (NEH), 93
National Historical Publications and Records Commission (NHPRC), 93
Negro Spiritual Heritage Keepers Project, The, 137
Neuenschwander, John, 109
non-profit status issue, 94
non-recurring expenses, 99

O
office staff, 54
Ogden, Catherine H., 63, 113
one-time expenses, 99
oral history
   defining, 11
   elements, 20
   as process, 12
   uses of, 132
Oral History Association (OHA)
   availability of guidelines, 42
   importance of guidelines, 12
   website, 42, 120
Oral History in the Digital Age (OHDA), 83
oral history programs, defining, 22
oral history project examples
   Advent House Ministries in Michigan, 135–36
   CCC in Minnesota, 136
   Cushman Motor Works in Nebraska, 27–28
   Greenwich Library in Connecticut, 63, 113
   In Our Own Words, 137
   Rocky Flats Cold War Museum, 129
oral history project examples, fictitious. *See* city fictitious project; historical society fictitious project; volunteer fictitious project
Oral History Project in Greenwich, Connecticut, 63, 113
oral history projects, defining, 22
orientation meetings, 62–63
outcomes
   from CCC in Minnesota project, 136
   importance of transcripts to, 129
   possible, 24, 25, 28
outreach plans, 50
overhead costs, described, 99–100

P
paperwork. *See* documentation
partnerships, obtaining donations from, 98
People Who Made It Work: A Centennial History of Cushman Motor Works, The, 28
performance evaluations, 97
performances in interviews, 110
per-interview costs, described, 100
Photograph and Memorabilia Receipt
   about, 76
   management notes, 76–77
   sample, 77–78
planning
   overview of, 13
   team members as project team

164 | Index

members, 24
time spent, 18
post-interview tasks
    immediate, 124
    Letter of Agreement for Repository processing requirements, 111, 125
    LOCKSS principle, 125
    project director responsibilities, 50
    See also entries beginning with *transcri;* preservation
preservation
    defining, 124
    importance of multiple copies, 125
    of interviews, 13
    long-term, 126–28
    steps, 125, 133–34
    terms used, 126
    See also entries beginning with *transcri;* repositories
pro bono expertise from professionals, 98
processing, 111–12, 125
processors (trained), 54–55
Project Design Statement
    for city fictitious project, 35–37
    for historical society fictitious project, 39–41
    as management guide, 29
    updating, 107, 113
    for volunteer fictitious project, 31–33
project director
    budget responsibilities, 102–3
    determination of paid and volunteer positions, 66
    equipment management responsibilities, 82, 84, 87–88
    external responsibilities, 48
    finding repository as priority, 120
    internal responsibilities, 49–50, 53, 107
    Legal Release Agreement responsibilities, 108
    outreach plan responsibilities, 50
    preservation responsibilities, 126, 128
    requirements, 48
    team management tips, 58
project focus, 49, 113

project forms. *See* forms
project scope, 29, 107
project wrap-up steps, 133–34
public face, project director as, 48
public relations
    celebrations as, 136–37
    community and, 134
    example of exhibit invitation, 135–36
    as responsibility of project director, 50

Q

questionable situations, dealing with, 109–10
quotations from interviews, use of, 110

R

recognition, 64
recorder maintenance technicians, 54
recording abstract, described, 126
recording equipment
    basic features of, 83
    choosing, 13, 83
    kit contents, 85–86
    maintenance guidelines, 87–88
    management responsibilities, 82, 86
    obtaining, 84, 98
    project director responsibilities, 50
    storage space for, 65
    training workshops, 88–90
    troubleshooting problems, 81–82
    using free computer programs, 84
    using iPhones as, 84
recordings
    long-term preservation, 126–27, 128
    wrap-up steps, 133
recording technicians, 53–54
remuneration policy, 110
repositories
    access and, 132, 133
    data files storage and maintenance by, 85
    finding appropriate, 118–19
    libraries as, 124
    negotiating with, 119
    overview of, 118
    processing requirements of, 111, 125
    project director responsibilities, 49

Index | 165

updating team and community
    about, 49
    web-hosted, 120, 122
reviews, as grant requirement, 97
Rocky Flats Cold War Museum project, 129

S

salvage oral history, defining, 95
sample forms
    Interviewee Biographical Profile Form, 70–72
    Interviewee Recommendation Form, 69
    Interview Summary, 73–74
    Interview Tracking Form, 75–76
    Legal Release Agreement, 44
    Legal Release Agreement (Restrictions), 45
    Letter of Agreement for Interviewer, 60
    Letter of Agreement for Repository, 121
    Letter of Agreement for Transcriber, 61
    Photograph and Memorabilia Receipt, 77–78
    time sheets, 62
slander, 109
sound quality, maximizing, 84
stability
    commitment to project duration by team members, 48, 55
    importance of, 49
storage space
    audio vs. video files, 85
    data files, 84–85
    security and accessibility of, 65
subpoenas, 110
support and funding. *See* funding; grants

T

team members
    bookkeepers/accountants, 54
    city fictitious project, 66–67
    collaboration among, 52
    consultants, 28, 55, 111
    historical society fictitious project, 67
    management tips, 58
    office staff, 54
    ongoing meetings with, 56
    optional, 55
    orientation meetings for, 62–63
    processors/catalogers (trained), 54–55
    project director, 48–50
    of projects with organizational affiliations, 67
    recorder maintenance technicians, 54
    recording technicians, 53–54
    recruiting, 55–58
    reviewing updated Project Design Statement with, 107
    roles needed, 51–52
    supervising, 49
    time sheets, 62
    volunteer fictitious project, 66
    See also interviewers; transcribers
thank yous, 64
time
    average, to complete each interview, 50
    commitment of team members, 48, 55, 57–58
    length of, to process each recorded hour, 111
    sheets, 62
    spent planning, 18
Toolkit, overview of, 11–13
training
    to assure consistent quality, 13
    interviewers, 117–18
    organizing and scheduling, 50
    recording equipment workshops, 88–90
    transcribers, 130–32
transcribers
    description of responsibilities, 57
    Letter of Agreement, sample, 61
    organizing and scheduling training of, 50
    responsibilities of, 53
    skilled needed by, 53
    training guides for, 131–32
    training workshops for, 130–31
transcribing
    described, 126
    interview logs and, 126

steps, 128–29
time needed per hour of interview, 111

transcripts
average number of pages, 111–12
described, 126
importance of, 129
for long-term preservation, 127

transparency, areas of, 108

U

Using Oral History in Community History Projects (Mercier and Buckendorf), 110

V

videographers, training on equipment of, 88–90
voice-activated equipment, 84
volunteer fictitious project
budget, 103
management notes, 30
overview of, 20, 30
processed interviews, 111–12
Project Design Statement, 31–33
project team members, 66
work space, 67

volunteers
documenting monetary value of, 67, 100–101
tips for working with, 63–64
typical number of interviews by, 111

W

web-hosted repositories, 120, 122
websites
budgeting for, 102
H-Oralhist, 120
OHA, 42, 120
uses of, 133
Wiskemann, Geneva Kebler, 25–26
work space
city fictitious project, 67
historical society fictitious project, 67
setting up, 65
volunteer fictitious project, 67

Y

Your Story and Mine: A Community of Hope (Advent House Ministries, Lansing, Michigan), 135–36

ABOUT THE AUTHORS

Barbara W. Sommer, M.A., has more than thirty-five years' experience in the oral history field. She has been principal investigator and director of more than twenty major oral history projects and has taught at the University of Nebraska-Lincoln, Nebraska Wesleyan University, and Vermilion Community College, MN. She is author of many key publications in the field, including, with Mary Kay Quinlan, *The Oral History Manual*, 2nd ed. (AltaMira Press, 2009) and with Quinlan and Charles E. Trimble, *The American Indian Oral History Manual: Making Many Voices Heard* (Left Coast Press, Inc., 2008). Her award-winning book *Hard Work and a Good Deal: The Civilian Conservation Corps in Minnesota* (Minnesota Historical Society Press, 2008) draws on oral history interviews about the Civilian Conservation Corps.

Nancy MacKay, MLIS, has been straddling the line between libraries and oral history for more than twenty years. As a librarian she has worked with special collections, cataloging, and music in various academic settings. As an oral historian she teaches, consults, advises, and writes about oral history, especially oral history and archives. She directed the oral history program at Mills College, from 2001-2011, and currently teaches library science and oral history at San Jose State University. Nancy is the author of *Curating Oral Histories* (Left Coast Press, Inc., 2007).

Mary Kay Quinlan, Ph.D., is an associate professor at the University of Nebraska-Lincoln in the College of Journalism and Mass Communications. She has held positions at the University of Maryland, and has served as president of the National Press Club. She is editor of the Oral History Association Newsletter and co-author with Barbara Sommer of *The Oral History Manual*, 2nd ed. (AltaMira Press, 2009), *Native American Veterans Oral History Manual* (Nebraska Foundation for the Preservation of Oral History, 2005), and *Discovering Your Connections to History* (AASLH, 2000). She is also a co-author with Sommer and Charles E. Trimble of *The American Indian Oral History Manual: Making Many Voices Heard* (Left Coast Press, Inc., 2008).